Nobody
Told
Me

A Guide for Pastors' Wives

By

Kay Cocklin

To Carolyn ~
Kay Cocklin
Col 2:8

PRESS

Nobody Told Me
A Guide for Pastors' Wives
by Kay Cocklin

Printed in the United States of America

ISBN 9781612153735

www.xulonpress.com

Dedication

This book is dedicated, first and foremost, to my family. I am so very appreciative for their love and support throughout the writing of this book. Not only did they encourage the process, but they agreed to let me share many of their embarrassing moments. Without them this book would not have been possible – and, it certainly would have been without a lot of humor!

Secondly, I dedicate the memories and experiences of <u>Nobody Told Me</u> to the New Cumberland First Church of God, New Cumberland, PA. Joel and I were blessed to serve an amazing congregation of people who loved us, and helped nurture us while we were learning how to minister to our first "flock". I can't find the words to express what this group of people means to both of us. Our ten years of ministry in this church still brings joy to our souls. I know that they continue to encourage, and love their present pastor, Charlie Zahora.

And lastly, I dedicate this book to all those who have gone before us in the ministry, who have set an example for us to follow. It is to honor those saints who have fought the good fight to bring the Truth of the Gospel to God's people. Specifically, I would like to dedicate this book to the first Pastor and wife team that I remember, the Reverend and Mrs. Paul Helm, who showed me that being a Christian could be fun. Also included in this dedication are the Reverend Dr. and Mrs. William Jackson, and the Reverend Dr. and Mrs. Kenneth Boldosser, who mentored Joel and me as we entered the ministry at the New Cumberland First Church of God. Included among these men and women of God are Chaplain (MAJ) and Mrs. Billy Goforth, Chaplain (COL) and Mrs. Marion Pember, Chaplain (COL) and Mrs. Alan Buckner, Chaplain (COL) and Mrs. Hal Roller, Chaplain (COL) and Mrs. Tom Lucas, and my husband, Chaplain (COL) Joel W. Cocklin. These men and their families sacrificed daily to bring Christ to soldiers around the world.

Table of Contents

Introduction

The focus of <u>Nobody Told Me</u> is to equip those who are starting on a journey of ministry. This book is a set of guidelines set forth to assist in preparing spouses for successful and rewarding ministerial lives. I realize that there are female pastors ministering in the churches, and therefore the spouse would be a male. For the sake of easier writing, I will refer to the Pastor's spouse as "wife", and use the pronouns "she" and "her". The guidelines were created to provide a basis for coping with the pressures and stresses of serving the church that can create stumbling blocks for a pastor and family.

The book consists of thirteen weeks of chapters. During those weeks you will be looking at:

An important aspect of this book will be the selection of a *Spiritual Armor Buddy*. Those of us who serve the Lord in ministry may face daily attack of various kinds. When we experience these attacks alone, we are very vulnerable to feelings of discouragement, doubt, and fear. Many organizations have realized the need for personal support – Alcoholics Anonymous is famous for finding success through a "buddy". I strongly encourage forming a bond with an *Armor Buddy*, which, hopefully, will give an outlet to express these events that can cause conflict.

Nobody Told Me was written specifically to equip the wife of the pastor in ministry. I have learned through my years as a ministerial spouse that pastoring God's people is not always an easy road. It was necessary to put on God's "battle gear" to protect against frustration, anger, bitterness, loneliness, fear, isolation, and worry. Don't get me wrong, the moments of joy, laughter, victory, and peace far exceeded the negative aspects of serving God. However, if you are not prepared for the experiences of attack, then they can destroy your ability to minister.

Unfortunately, we are seeing a rising number of pastors and families who have crumbled under the weight of the negative aspects of church ministry. It is my desire to have some part in providing the necessary equipment to step into this calling of God with confidence

– knowing that The God who called you to this adventure has not left you without protection against the "slings and arrows".

God has given us the equipment to guard ourselves against the times of attack. Ephesians 6:11-18 is very clear that those who serve the Lord need to "gear up" to protect themselves in order to minister. Just as a soldier needs to make use of every bit of body armor to withstand the enemy's advance, we need to put on each item of God's armor for our protection against the enemy's presence in our circumstances.

We will be looking at the scripture concerning "The Armor of God", and various other passages from scripture that we can place in our mind, and on our body for the purpose of having a successful ministry.

I look forward to sharing this walk with you and assisting you as you enter this new phase of your life with confidence, trusting that God has given you guidelines on how to find a rewarding life spent ministering to His people.

"It Ain't Heavy, It's My Armor"

Chapter One

using

Ephesians 6:11-18

Chapter One

It Ain't Heavy, It's My Armor

G od realized when He called people to minister to His creation that they would need reassurances of His continued presence in their lives. Throughout the Old and New Testaments, God continually reminds us that He will be the sustaining force that we can count on each day. It was made clear during the three-year ministry of His Son, Jesus, that each new day will bring possibilities, challenges, joy, discouragement, celebration, and agony. Paul writes of these things in 2 Corinthians 4:7-11:

> But we have this treasure in earthen vessels, so that the surpassing greatness of the power will be of God and not from ourselves; we are afflicted in every way, but not crushed; perplexed, but not despairing; persecuted, but not forsaken; struck down, but not destroyed; always carrying about in the body the dying of Jesus, so that the life of Jesus also may be

manifested in our body. For we who live are constantly being delivered over to death for Jesus' sake, so that the life of Jesus also may be manifested in our mortal flesh (NASB, 1498).

Scripture instructs us exactly what God has prepared for us so that we can successfully handle each aspect of church ministry. Read through the verses from Ephesians. You may need to read through several times. Feel free to underline, circle, or highlight those words or phrases that tend to grab your attention.

Ephesians 6: 10 – 18 (NIV)

Finally, be strong in the Lord and in his mighty power. Put on the full armor of God so that you can take your stand against the devil's schemes. For our struggle is not against flesh and blood, but against the rulers, against the authorities, against the powers of this dark world and against the spiritual forces of evil in the heavenly realms. Therefore put on the full armor of God, so that when the day of evil comes, you may be able to stand your ground, and after you have done everything, to stand. Stand firm then, with the *belt of truth* buckled around your waist, with the *breastplate of righteousness* in place, And with your feet fitted with the readiness that comes from the gospel of peace. In addition to all this, take up the *shield of faith*, with which you can extinguish all the flaming arrows of the evil one. Take the *helmet of salvation* and the *sword of the Spirit* which is the *word of God*. And *pray in the Spirit* on all occasions with all kinds of prayers and requests. With this in mind, be alert and always keep on praying for all the saints" (NIV, [1924, italics and underline mine]).

BATTLEMIND was first developed by Walter Reed Army Institute of Research during the deployment and redeployment of soldiers to Iraq and Afghanistan. These guidelines were created to increase the resiliency of the family after deployment into a battlefield situation. BATTLEMIND has shown widespread success in preparing the soldier, spouse, and family for separation and the problems that arise due to the stresses of the deployment.

Nobody told Me was created for a similar purpose: to increase the resiliency of the pastor's family during ministry. It is my sincere hope that these guidelines will prepare the spouse and family for the trials that can surface during ministry.

What is "resiliency"? It is the ability to bounce back to a previous state – similar to a rubber band. We stretch the rubber band and when we release it, the band returns to its original shape. Resilience in our lives is much the same. However, many times when we "bounce back" after an experience in our lives, we have changed slightly.

Change doesn't necessarily have to be bad – it is just different than before. When we experience positive and negative situations, then we adjust and learn.

As with the rubber band, if it is stretched too often, it will not return to its original shape. And, if it is stretched too far, the rubber band will break. These two scenarios are what I hope you can avoid as you minister. The perfect and ideal scenario is to be stretched just so far, and return to the original shape, with minor changes. It is not always possible to control how far, and how hard we are stretched as individuals, but God has given us protection against those situations that would break us.

Just as soldiers wear specific battle gear to guard against injury, Christians have "battle gear" to wear as they venture out to spread the Good News. Ephesians 6:11-18 tells us that there are six items that we are to put on for protection:

The Belt of Truth

The Breastplate of Righteousness

The Shield of Faith

The Sword of the Spirit which is the Word of God

The Helmet of Salvation

Prayer

That raises important questions: Why do we need protection? What do you believe about the presence of evil in the world and its affect on you? The presence of evil in the world is directly related to the presence of Satan. We must understand that we are not protected against the influence of Satan. We are more vulnerable to his temptations when we are frustrated, lonely, and feeling overwhelmed by our circumstances. The only protection we have is to stay grounded in Christ, scripture, and the fellowship of believers.

In Ephesians 6:13, it says that you put on the armor of God so that "when the day of evil comes you will be able to stand your ground". In your mind, how do you interpret "the day of evil"? Is this a one-time occurrence, or is it possible to have many days of evil during your lifetime? According to what we believe, "the day of evil" will be when Satan tries to take control; however, each major situation you encounter can present the same "day of evil". Possessing and wearing the armor of God will allow you to triumph over devastating circumstances in your life.

Pastors and their families are especially susceptible to attacks from Satan. The enemy's purpose is to seek our weak and vulnerable areas, and create feelings that tear us down. How many times have you noticed in your life that when an amazing, God-created and God-filled moment occurs, not long afterwards the attacks begin from other sources? Scripture reveals in I Peter 5:8, "Be self-controlled and alert. Your enemy the devil prowls around looking for someone to devour." (NIV) As my husband's mother used to say, "The devil doesn't care which end of the bridge he knocks you off of!" We used to laugh at her saying, but have since realized the truth in her words. Satan enjoys seeing us suffer, and he abhors seeing us joyful and bringing people to Christ. He will double his attack when things are going well in our ministry.

Each of us has strengths and weaknesses in our life and faith. It is extremely important to evaluate ourselves, and honestly observe those strengths and weaknesses. We find that if we allow those weak areas to remain, Satan is granted an entrance into our being and is able to create chaos. It is like knowing that there is a crack in the wall, a flood is coming, and we do nothing to fix the crack. The water comes and finds that small opening and flows in at a trickle; slowly, but surely, the crack widens, and the wall eventually breaks. When we are aware of weaknesses in our lives, we must turn to God to guide us in repairing that weak spot, and thus remove any possible entry spot for Satan.

CUES THAT INDICATE LACK OF RESILIENCY

AND STRESS

God has placed cues in our body that signal when we are stressed and trying to cope with negative situations. It is very important to keep a close tab on your mental physical, spiritual health, and well-being.

⟩ Those cues are:

   *feeling depressed and down

   *isolating yourself, or withdrawing

   *feeling angry, tense, hostile, irritable, and/or resentful

   *difficulty sleeping or sleeping too much

   *significant appetite changes

   *not finding fun in things previously enjoyed

   *using over-the-counter medications, illegal drugs or alcohol to

   cope

   *taking out frustrations on others

   *suicidal or homicidal thinking, intent or actions

   *family, coworkers, or friends tell you that you need help

      (Walter Reed Army Institute of Research)

Don't become defensive if someone suggests you may need help in

dealing with a situation, and don't be afraid to ask for help!

   During the week ahead please take a closer look at yourself, and

which pieces of God's armor you have already selected to wear.

Determine which areas of your life are still unprotected. Use your journal pages to write about this, and work towards applying the rest of the "battle gear" to your body. "For our struggle is not against flesh and blood, but against the rulers, against the authorities, against the powers of this dark world and against the spiritual forces of evil in the heavenly realms" (Ephesians 6:12, [NASB]).

Daily Journal – Consider which parts of the Armor of God you already use to protect yourself. Write about those and then honestly determine which parts of the "battle gear" are missing.

MONDAY

TUESDAY

WEDNESDAY

THURSDAY

FRIDAY

SATURDAY

SUNDAY

"GOD CALLS"

Chapter Two

Using

**2 Cor. 6:14; Romans 12:6;
1 Sam. 3:1-10;
Isa. 6:1-13; and 2 Tim. 4:1-5**

Chapter Two

God Calls

It seems like it has been an eternity since my husband received the call to enter the ministry. And then, at the same time, it seems like it has been only a blink of an eye. For some people the call from God is an easy call to answer. But, for others, the voice of the Lord is an intruder.

Joel was in his freshman year at Findlay College (now the University of Findlay). He was studying to be a Physical Education teacher – he has always excelled in sports. During that year, he began to feel uneasy about his major, and attributed that to his lack of height and weight – 5' 11" and 135 pounds.

During the second semester of his freshman year, Joel switched his major to Mathematics, his second favorite subject. There was no feeling of satisfaction in what he was studying, but he continued to press on with his education. There was a nagging sense that he was not doing what he was supposed to be doing.

The summer between his freshman and sophomore year Joel was restless, irritable, and argumentative. He was losing sleep and weight. It was on an evening, after a date, that Joel and I were sitting on the couch in my home. He was just so sad, and frustrated. After months of watching him like this, I asked him to share with me what was wrong. He told me that he felt God was calling him to the ministry, but he knew that choice was impossible. He had a scholarship that required him to go back home after graduation, and teach for three years, or he would have to pay the money back. Joel knew he would lose that scholarship, and he had no idea how he would obtain the money to continue his education.

After several hours of discussion (arguing?) and praying, the decision was made to answer God's call to the ministry, and let

God deal with the issue of the scholarship money. It was amazing to watch the change that occurred in Joel after he accepted God's call. He was able to sleep, eat, carry on a normal conversation, and he was just pleasant to be around again. God provides when you are obedient to His will. Joel never had to repay the scholarship money, and each year his college fees were covered through various kind donors.

Everyone experiences God's call to ministry in a different way. For some, it is an easy answer. It is what they had hoped, dreamed, and planned for their whole life. But, for others, it comes as a struggle – this was not what *they* had planned.

You are most likely reading this book because your husband is preparing for the ministry, or is already pastoring in one way or another. I want you to look at your Spouse's call from God and think about what type of reaction occurred. It is important to ask him to tell you his story, if the two of you were not together when your Spouse received God's call. The process of answering the call is an integral part of his ministry. Over many years of ministry, the pastor returns to that moment for reassurance that this is God's purpose, and role for his life.

The big question for you is: Were you called also? Is it necessary that the Pastor's spouse be called of God? You may be feeling slightly uneasy at this point, and that is ok. Have you thought about this question before? Did you experience a call to be the spouse of a Pastor? Does this type of call exist?

What does scripture say about the calling of the spouse? Unfortunately, the Bible does not address whether God calls the spouse of the Pastor. However, there is support in 2 Corinthians 6:14,"Do not be yoked together with the unbelievers. For what do righteousness and wickedness have in common" (NIV, 1892). God is very clear that in a marriage both must have a faith in Jesus Christ.

Let's look at the whole aspect of "being yoked". Get a mental image of two oxen that are yoked together. The load they are pulling is large, and very heavy. The yoke itself is biting into the shoulders of the oxen. One ox is well-built and muscular; whereas, the other ox is not full-grown, his muscles are not evident, and the yoke does not even rest on his shoulders. As the oxen begin to pull their load, it is quite evident that they are unevenly matched. Their path is not straight and only one ox is bearing the burden of the load.

So it is with marriage. Unless the husband and wife are "evenly yoked", then the marriage will not go forward in a straight path, and one of the partners must bear the burdens for both. Ministry to God's people depends on unity: a unified front between the two that are yoked together. This "unified front" is a common faith in Jesus Christ as Lord and Savior.

The questions that naturally follow that discussion are: If I am called, too, what then does God expect of me? How much will be required of me as we enter the ministry? What if I don't feel comfortable speaking or praying in public? Can I have my own occupation? Basically, the question is: WHAT WILL IT COST ME? Those are all great questions, and you are not the first to ask them. I would be worried if you were not asking those questions! Each person has to answer the questions after much thought and prayer. Also, God answers each person differently, according to the gifts He has given them.

God asks no more from you, as the spouse of the Pastor than He does of the rest of His followers. He has given each person gifts to be shared in the family of God, and that is what He requires of you. From Romans 12:6, we all have different gifts: prophecy, service, teaching, encouragement, generous giving, leadership, and mercy. We must each determine the gifts we possess from God, and He will use them as we minister side-by-side with our spouse.

I was privileged to be present when the daughter of Billy Graham, Anne Graham Lotz, spoke to our women's group at Fort Bragg, North Carolina. She was not speaking about her father's ministry, but she did refer to her parents. Ms. Lotz made a comment that has stayed with me in looking at my role as a Pastor's spouse. She said that her mother, Ruth, created a haven of rest in the home. When her husband returned after a day of facing many tough moments in ministering, he entered a peaceful environment to be able to recuperate and refresh. What an amazing gift she gave her husband while she was part of his ministry. She served an important role – it may not have been out front, and noticed by his congregation, but it allowed him to rejuvenate to continue the next day to save souls for the Kingdom!

Looking at Scripture

Read this scripture - Samuel's Call – I Samuel 3:1-10

The LORD Calls Samuel

The boy Samuel ministered before the LORD under Eli. In those days the word of the LORD was rare; there were not many visions. One night Eli, whose eyes were becoming so weak that he could barely see, was lying down in his usual place. The lamp of God had not yet gone out, and Samuel was lying down in the temple of the LORD, where the ark of God was. Then the LORD called Samuel. Samuel answered, "Here I am." And he ran to Eli and said, "Here I am; you called me." But Eli said, "I did not call; go back and lie down." So he went and lay down. Again the LORD called, "Samuel!" And Samuel got up and went to Eli and said, "Here I am; you called me." "My son," Eli said, "I did not call; go back and lie down." Now Samuel did not yet know the LORD : The word of the LORD had not yet been revealed to him. The LORD called Samuel a third time, and Samuel got up and went to Eli and said, "Here I am; you called me." Then Eli realized that the LORD was calling the boy. So Eli told Samuel, "Go and lie down, and if he calls you, say, 'Speak, LORD, for your servant is listening.' "So Samuel went and lay down in his place. The LORD came and stood there, calling as at the other times, "Samuel! Samuel!" Then Samuel said, "Speak, for your servant is listening" (NIV, 402).

Like Samuel, God may have been calling us for a long time, and we mistakenly thought the call was from somewhere or someone else. Three times Samuel believed that it was Eli who was trying to get his attention. Unfortunately, we may not always realize when God is trying to speak to us.

Eli realized after the third time that it was God's voice that was waking Samuel in the middle of the night. It was Eli who told Samuel to go back to the temple, and wait for God to speak to him again. There are times when it may be necessary for God to use someone else to tell us that He is calling, and trying to get our attention.

THINKING POINT: *Why is it easier to hear (recognize) what God is trying to tell others, and so difficult to hear, and understand when He speaks to us?*

Samuel obeyed, returned to his resting place, and when God called the fourth time, Samuel responded and received the message from God. In verse 11, God tells Samuel, "See, I am about to do something in Israel that will make the ears of everyone who hears it tingle." When God called you and your spouse, He said the same thing.

The message Samuel was to give to God's people was not a pleasant one! Samuel was afraid to tell Eli the message he had received from God, because it was a message of retribution for past sins. There will also be times when your spouse will be called by God to bring messages to His people that are not pleasant ones.

• **THINKING POINT**: *What would your reaction be if God told you to be the messenger of His anger to a group of people?*

Read the scripture - Isaiah's Call – Isaiah 6:1-13

In the year of King Uzziah's death I saw the Lord sitting on a throne, lofty and exalted, with the train of His robe filling the temple. Seraphim stood above Him, each having six wings: with two he covered his face, and with two he covered his feet, and with two he flew. And one called out to another and said, "Holy, Holy, Holy, is the Lord of hosts, the whole earth is full of His glory."And the foundations of the thresholds trembled at the voice of him who called out, while the temple was filling with smoke. Then I said, "Woe is me, for I am ruined! Because I am a man of unclean lips, And I live among a people of unclean lips; For my eyes have seen the King, the Lord of hosts. "Then one of the seraphim flew to me with a burning coal in his hand, which he had taken from the altar with tongs. He touched my mouth with it and said, "Behold, this has touched your lips; and your iniquity is taken away and your sin is forgiven."Then I heard the voice of the Lord, saying, "Whom shall I send, and who will go for us?" Then I said, "Here am I. Send me!"He said, "Go, and tell this people: 'Keep on listening, but do not perceive; Keep on looking, but do not understand. "Render the hearts of this people insensitive, Their ears dull, And their eyes dim, Otherwise they might see with their eyes, Hear with their ears, Understand with their hearts, And return and be healed. "Then I said, "Lord, how long?" And He answered, "Until cities are devastated and without inhabitant, Houses are without people and the land is utterly desolate, "The Lord has removed men far away, and the forsaken places are many in the midst of the land."Yet there will be a tenth portion in it, and it will again be subject to burning, like a terebinth or an oak whose stump remains when it is felled. The holy seed is its stump" (NASB, 889).

When God's call went out to Isaiah, he believed that he was

not worthy to bring God's mission to the world. In verse 5, Isaiah

says that he has "unclean lips". But God sent an angel, and cleansed

Isaiah's lips so there would be no excuse for his refusal to participate in God's mission.

⬥ **THINKING POINT**: *What excuses do you use when God calls for*
your help in completing His mission?

After the excuse for Isaiah's involvement in God's mission is
removed, Isaiah responds, "Here am I! Send me!" This was a very
bold statement for a man who had just told God that he was not
worthy! God proceeds to give Isaiah the message, and like Samuel,
God gives a message that is not very positive. Isaiah reacts the way
most of us would – he asks a very human question: How long is this
going to last?

⬥ **THINKING POINT**: *Does this reaction sound familiar?*
Unpleasant situations cause us to ask the same thing.

Do you suppose that sometimes we respond too quickly, "Here
am I! Send me!" Once we hear the message God wishes us to give,

our response to His request is, "How long do you want me to do this?"

Read the scripture - Paul's Charge to Timothy: 2 Timothy 4:1-5

In the presence of God and of Christ Jesus, who will judge the living and the dead, and in view of his appearing and his kingdom, I give you this charge: Preach the Word; be prepared in season and out of season; correct, rebuke and encourage—with great patience and careful instruction. For the time will come when men will not put up with sound doctrine. Instead, to suit their own desires, they will gather around them a great number of teachers to say what their itching ears want to hear. They will turn their ears away from the truth and turn aside to myths. But you, keep your head in all situations, endure hardship, do the work of an evangelist, discharge all the duties of your ministry" (NIV, 1967).

Paul's writing to Timothy could be considered a letter to all those entering the ministry. He reminds Timothy of the changes in the world of faith, and gives him advice on how to counter the sins of the people.

Paul tells Timothy that he is to "correct, rebuke, and encourage" the people as he preaches God's word. He was pointing out to

Timothy that his duty was to point the people away from the "philosophies of this world" (Col 3:8), and direct them in God's truth.

THINKING POINT: *Which issues do you feel Timothy would be focusing on today as he preached God's word?*

SUMMARY: What personally jumps out at you from this passage?

_____

_____

Daily Journal – Use this week to write about the three issues we dealt with in this session: Hearing and answering God's call; using excuses to avoid taking God's messages; sharing a message from God that is counter to popular thought.

MONDAY

TUESDAY

WEDNESDAY

THURSDAY

FRIDAY

SATURDAY

SUNDAY

"Follow Me?" Does That Mean I Need to Move?

Chapter Three

Using

Matthew 28:19-20 and Various Old and New Testament Verses

Chapter Three

"Follow Me?" Does That Mean I Have to Move?

T here are many situations in life that are scary. Flying, to me, brings on anxiety attacks! One really frightening landing in the Miami airport was all it took to traumatize me for the rest of my life. My palms start to sweat just to think about it. And, no matter how much I tell myself that flying is safer than driving, my mind just doesn't buy it. I've never especially enjoyed visits to the dentist either. Needles and drills don't belong in the mouth. I am sure that you could add many experiences to this list that cause you to feel much the same way. For many of you, the idea of leaving your hometown, and moving to some strange, and unfamiliar location would rank right up there with monsters under the bed! It is not easy to pull up roots, pack up all of your worldly possessions, and relocate the family to unknown territories. But, sometimes, that's exactly what God wants, and expects you to do.

Joel and I were very happy serving God in New Cumberland. We were witnessing the tremendous power of His Spirit in the church. Many times we made the comment to each other, and to members of the church, that we could see ourselves staying there for the next twenty-five years. So, you can imagine our shock when we realized that God was indicating to us, in very subtle ways, that He had a "new adventure" in mind for us! Adding to that revelation was the fact that He wanted us to become part of the Army! You must understand that Joel spent his seven years of higher education avoiding the military draft, because that meant going to Viet Nam! And now, God expected him to voluntarily raise his right hand to serve his country, and God? Here was my monster under the bed, and it was terrifying me.

Joel reported for active duty in June 1982, and by the end of July, we had moved to Fort Campbell, Kentucky, just northwest of Nashville, Tennessee. We moved into "quarters" (the Army term for our house) by the middle of August. I remember sitting in the kitchen soon after we had received our furniture from Pennsylvania. The children were outside playing with new friends, Joel was working in his office at Chapel 11, and I was alone. As I drank a cup of coffee, tears rolled down my cheeks, I bowed my head, and thought, "Lord, what have we done??? Joel is a Soldier. They could send him wherever they want. The Army has complete control over our lives. How could You do this to us?"

And God said, "Kay, I am the One who has control, not the Army – you are in My hands. Trust Me to lead you in this commitment you have made to minister to soldiers, and their families. I will not leave you alone in this new adventure that you have begun!" I would love to tell you that I finished that cup of coffee, got up, and never had another worry about the move we had made, but I would be lying. What consumed my mind was what we had left behind in

New Cumberland. I missed what had been familiar to me: my role as a Pastor's wife, my church family, my friends, and our extended family that lived in Maryland, and Pennsylvania. All I lived for was the thought of going back for a visit at Thanksgiving.

What I discovered that Thanksgiving of 1982 was that people change! I had changed because of my experiences. I realized that much of what I was remembering, and longing for, no longer seemed important. My life had taken on new dimensions, and I had one of those "AH-HAH" moments! God had put us exactly where we were supposed to be, and I couldn't wait to get back to Fort Campbell to willingly submit to our new calling and ministry.

When you say "yes" to the calling of the Spirit, God knows where He wants you to serve – and, that may not be where you are living at the moment. I have talked to so many men and women who have answered the call to the ministry, but refuse to "uproot the family". In giving that response, you have placed limitations on how God can use you. Throughout scripture, when God called someone, the next word from Him was, "Go. Feed my sheep". God's call requires action.

The most important piece of the adventure of serving God is that HE GOES WITH YOU! God prepares the path for you. Trust is evident when you are able to say to the Lord, with courage and conviction -"Then I heard the voice of the Lord, saying, 'Whom shall I send, and who will go for Us?' Then I said, *'Here am I. Send me"* (NASB, 890 [emphasis mine]).

A very large concern when facing a move is the impact the relocation will have on the children. The most important factor in creating a positive experience for your children centers on your attitude about the change. If you anticipate the move with a positive attitude, then your children will respond in the same way. Every time Joel received orders for a permanent change of station (PCS) we would get out the map, find where it was, and point out everything that would be available in the area to see and do. We always referred to our moves as a "new adventure" and approached it with excitement. Each child was always allowed to pack their own backpack for the travels with their "prized" possessions. Today, if you were to ask our children their opinion on moving ten times in their life, they would tell you that it was the best decision their father ever made.

Kelly was just beginning her freshmen year at the University of Kansas. She was in her seat for her first class, and the professor said that she wanted each student to introduce themselves, and give the name of their hometown. Kelly told us that she sat there wondering what her response would be to the second part of the question. She listened as each student shared their name, and talked about where they had grown up. Finally, it was her turn. She said that she took a deep breath, gave her name, and then it went something like this: "I don't really have a hometown. I've lived all over the United States, and even in Germany. My parents live at Fort Riley, Kansas, right now, so I guess that's my hometown!" After class, as Kelly was leaving, the professor stopped her, and asked if she had a few minutes to come to her office. Wondering what she possibly could have done wrong on her first day of class, she followed the professor. The instructor asked Kelly how she could be so comfortable not having a hometown. She wondered how Kelly could have possibly been okay with moving ten times. There was no hesitation when she answered the professor. Kelly said that moving had been an adventure, and that she had friends all over the world. She had seen things that most students only knew from textbooks. What made her response so special to Joel and I, was that she credited us with giving her the right attitude to face such an ever-changing environment. God had kept His promise to us from the very beginning that He would never leave us, and that He had prepared the path for us. All we had to do was "go", and the rest was up to Him.

Looking At Scripture

The Bible is filled with examples of how God has required followers of His to leave that which is familiar, and move to a new location. The very first move was made by Adam and Eve, in Genesis 3:23-24. They had no choice to remain in the Garden of Eden. This first move was the result of disobedience to God. But, let's take a look at references to relocating as a means of furthering God's Kingdom.

After the destruction by flood, and the rehabitation of the land by the descendents of Noah, we read about a man called Abram. His story of being called by God to move from his home is located in Genesis 12.

> Now the LORD said to Abram, "Go forth from your country, and from your relatives and from your father's house, to the land which I will show you; and I will make you a great nation, and I will bless you, and make your name great; and so you shall be a blessing; and I will bless those who bless you, and the one who curses you I will curse and in you all the families of the earth will be blessed." ***So Abram went forth as the LORD had spoken to him*** (15, NASB, emphasis mine).

Read this scripture several times, and as you do so, put your name in the first verse instead of the name "Abram".

THINKING POINT: *We know nothing about Abram before Genesis 12, except that he was married to Sarai, his father was Terah, and* they had settled in the land of Haran. What command was Abram given, and how did he respond to the command of the Lord?

_____

_____

_____

_____

_____

_____

• **<u>THINKING POINT</u>**: _Have you received a command from the Lord to leave the familiar territory - friends, family, the home of your youth – and move to a strange new location? What was your response to God's command?_

_____

_____

_____

_____

_____

Reading Scripture

Exodus 3:1-4:20 <u>MOSES</u>

Read the story concerning Moses and the call he received from God to return to Egypt to rescue the Israelite people from slavery. I want you to notice several things as you read:

- What was Moses asked to do?
- What was Moses' response to God's command?
- How many times did Moses try to give excuses that would prevent him from doing what God required him to do?
- What was God's reaction to Moses in Chapter 4:14?
- What was the final response by Moses to God's call?

Was it possible that you saw yourself in Moses' response to the need of God? We want to think that if God asked us to speak His word to a particular group of people, our response would be to go, even if it meant leaving everything we knew and loved. What we have to understand is that Moses had found a place of peace and rest in Midian. He had married, and was tending sheep for his father-in-law. BUT, God does not call us to be comfortable! When you feel yourself getting comfortable in your position of service to God, maybe it's time to listen for that voice of God, because He just may shake things up for you! Don't be afraid to answer that call from your Father in Heaven. Trust him to fill every need you have when you faithfully respond to Him.

THINKING POINT: *What excuses have you used with God when He has specifically called you to minister to a specific issue, or group of people? Has He ever asked you to "go", and you refused?*

_____

_____

_____

_____

_____

_____

Ruth 1 – 4 <u>RUTH</u>

Read the book of Ruth, especially to discover how relocation affected her lifestyle, and future. Consider when reading these chapters the impact on biblical history had Ruth not followed Naomi to Bethlehem. Why is Ruth important in the New Testament story?

⟩ **THINKING POINT**: *There is no mention in the book of Ruth that God prompted her to follow Naomi to Bethlehem. How do you know that this was part of God's will for her life and for us?*

_____

_____

_____

_____

_____

_____

_____

❧ **THINKING POINT**: *List the ways that God led Ruth, through Naomi, throughout the four chapters of the book of Ruth.*

_____

_____

_____

_____

_____

_____

Jonah 1 – 4 JONAH

The ultimate example of running from the command of God was the story of Jonah. God called Jonah to leave his home, and travel to the land of the Ninevites, preach repentance, and save the people from their sinful ways. According to scripture Jonah made no attempt to respond to the command – he just left Tarshish, and fled to Joppa. Read the account of Jonah and his flight from God's call.

THINKING POINT: *Why did Jonah expend so much energy in running away from what God commanded him to do?*

_____

_____

_____

_____

_____

_____

THINKING POINT: *What would be your response if God commanded you to go to a Muslim country, and preach acceptance of the Lord? Maybe He has called you to leave your present job, and community – what has been your response?*

_____

_____

_____

_____

_____

Mark 1:16-20 PETER, JAMES, AND JOHN

Our final look at how individuals responded to the command of God to leave what was familiar to them, is the call of the first three disciples. We'll end the way we began this chapter. Abram gave God no excuses – there was no hesitation when the Lord told him to leave his land, and go to a territory that He would show him. GOD DIDN'T EVEN GIVE HIM THE NAME OF THE PLACE, BUT ABRAM STILL WENT!! Read this account of Jesus' interaction with Peter, James, and John.

THINKING POINT: *The verses in Mark's gospel tell us that Jesus asked the fishermen to follow him. What was the response of these men mentioned in the verses of Chapter 1? Did they ask where? Were they told for how long? Was there an inquiry as to how much they would be paid? Did they even know who Jesus was?*

_____

_____

_____

_____

_____

_____

THINKING POINT: *What keeps us from freely going where God commands us to go? How do we get to the point where we can respond like Abram, and the first three disciples? What did they possess that we might lack?*

_____

_____

_____

_____

_____

_____

Matthew 26:26-46 JESUS IN GETHSEMANE

The ultimate submission to going where God commanded was in the response of Jesus to the commitment of the cross. We see the agony of the Son of God as He prayed in the Garden of Gethsemane.

Take a few moments to read the verses located in Chapter 26.

THINKING POINT: *How do you know that Jesus struggled with the command that God had given Him of going to the Cross? No other command of God given to mankind has had the depth of total commitment than this path to the crucifixion. How was Jesus able to "go" to the cross and bear the suffering, pain and agony that He did?*

_____

_____

_____

_____

_____

_____

THINKING POINT: *What was the final command of Christ to His followers before leaving their midst? As you read Matthew 28:19-*

20, what is the first word in verse 19? Christ did not say, "Stay in your hometown, where your friends and family are – be comfortable and safe." What is your response to the words of Christ in this passage?

_____

_____

_____

_____

_____

_____

Daily Journal – Meditate this week on how God may be calling you, and your spouse to a new and challenging ministry. Do you find yourself giving excuses for why you cannot do what He is asking you to do? Look at each scripture passage from this chapter, and each example of ways to response when God commands you to "Go!" Consider whether you prefer to remain in the familiar, instead of giving the response, "Here am I. Send me."

MONDAY

TUESDAY

WEDNESDAY

THURSDAY

FRIDAY

SATURDAY

SUNDAY

"The Pastor's Wife Stereotype"

Chapter Four

Using

Various Scriptures
From the Old and New Testament

Chapter Four

"The Pastor's Wife Stereotype"

Three little words, "The Pastor's Wife", can conjure up a variety of mental images. Just take a minute, close your eyes, and form a picture in your mind. I can only guess that you envision a woman in a dress, wearing sensible shoes and glasses, her hair is in a bun, and there is an unending smile on her face. Possibly, she is even carrying a Bible in one hand, and a covered dish for the homebound parishioner in the other. For some, that is exactly what the pastor's wife should look like. Fortunately, we have moved beyond that stereotype – she still should be moderately dressed, not too many piercings (smile), and have a pleasant attitude.

I need to stop here, and explain what you would have seen in me at the time that Joel was called into the ministry. We were twenty years old, and in college. I had attended Cosmetology School in Frederick, Maryland, and had graduated from there before attending college. I truly enjoyed "messing" with my hair, and therefore no one, least of all Joel, was ever sure what color, or what style my hair would be! I minored in Art at Findlay, and being very "right-brained", was a free spirit – and I still am to some degree. I loved the mini-skirt era because I was tall, skinny, and had great legs. Are you getting a picture of a pastor's wife here?????? Oh – lest I forget – I was also a smoker! I just flunked the final exam for being the perfect pastor's wife! I had two things going in my favor: 1.) I loved God with all of my heart, soul, mind, and strength, and, 2.) I had asked Jesus into my heart to be my Lord, and my Savior.

What you must realize, before you go any further, is that God does not judge by the outer characteristics, but by the inner heart and spirit. He sees the potential in each of us when we submit to His leading and His call. I could never have made myself what I am today – it was only when I said, "Well, God, you called Joel into the ministry. I love him, and I plan on marrying him. If I'm going to be the wife of a pastor, then You have a lot of work to do on me, so that I will be acceptable."

I laugh now when I remember what I thought would be required of me in order to be acceptable and suitable! I had that stereotypical idea of what I would have to give up. I would no longer be able to color my hair, or cut it in the newest style. I would go gray "gracefully", and wear it in a French twist – a more modern version of a bun! I wasn't sure what the church members would think of pierced ears on their pastor's wife – I'd have to wait and see. Of course, the mini-skirts would have to go, and I'd get used to wearing dresses to mid-calf. Definitely, I would have to curb my free-spirited attitude, and become more "sedate", while still keeping my friendliness.

What I discovered as we entered the ministry was that none of the above was required. The only thing that changed about me was that I gave up smoking, "cold-turkey", in August 1970. The congregation loved me as I was, and accepted all of my quirks, and free-spirited attitude. The New Cumberland First Church of God opened their arms, and loved me exactly as I was – colored hair, pierced ears, and mini-skirts.

Biblical Examples of Those Called by God

It would be putting it mildly to say that I was shocked to discover, as an adult, that Jonah was not a nice person! Have you ever read the **whole** story??? My Sunday school teachers left out a very important part about Jonah. I was taught the following facts about Jonah:

- He was called by God for the specific mission of saving the Ninevites.

- Jonah ran away, and boarded a ship to escape God's request.

- Jonah is tossed overboard and swallowed by a whale.

- Jonah cries out to God to rescue him.

- Jonah is rescued by God, and the whale spits him out.

- Jonah goes to Nineveh, and saves the people.

(And that's where my Sunday school teachers stopped!) Maybe they thought I couldn't handle "the rest of the story".

At age forty-eight, I was teaching Bible to the ninth through twelfth grade students at a Christian school in upstate New York. The book of the Bible being taught was the book of Jonah. When I got to the last chapter, and read Jonah's reaction to the salvation of the Ninevites, I was in shock. It reads, "But it greatly displeased Jonah and he became angry" (NASB, 1197). WHAT? Jonah helped God save a whole nation of people, and he was angry? Obviously, God can use people that we would never choose. Likewise, even if I don't understand what it is that God requires of me, He's still going to use me.

You may be looking at yourself right now, asking God what in the world He saw in you that He chose you to be the wife of a pastor. There may be a huge feeling of inadequacy running rampant throughout your body. If not, praise God – you don't need this chapter. But for the vast majority of us, we spend way too much time and energy worrying about these things: why did He choose me, what if I am not capable, what if I am a failure, what if I embarrass my husband, and the list of questions can go on forever.

BUT – you may be certain of one thing, "For I am confident of this very thing, that He who began a good work in you will perfect it until the day of Christ Jesus" (NASB, 1521). When God calls you there is absolutely no way that He will not complete His mission in you. The Father does not choose us, and then abandon us. The "liar" loves to stir up feelings of doubt among those who are trying to do God's will. This is the time when we grab our Belt of Truth from our battle gear, and strap it on tightly. When we are wearing that piece of God's armor, then we will go forward with trust and confidence.

Looking At Scripture

I want you to spend some time looking at a few descriptions about women/wives in the Bible. After reading each reference, write a few words that have been used to describe them.

- Genesis 2:23 -The man said, "This is now bone of my bones, and flesh of my flesh; She shall be called Woman, because she was taken out of Man" (NASB, 3).

_____

_____

_____

_____

- Ruth 3: 11 - Now, my daughter, do not fear. I will do for you whatever you ask, for all my people in the city know that you are a woman of excellence (NASB, 353).

_____

_____

_____

_____

- Proverbs 11:16 – A gracious woman attains honor, and ruthless men attain riches.

_____

_____

_____

_____

- Proverbs 25:24 – It is better to live in a corner of the roof than in a house shared with a contentious woman (NASB, 854).

_____

_____

_____

_____

- Proverbs 5:18 – Let your fountain be blessed, and rejoice in the wife of your youth (NASB, 828).

_____

_____

_____

_____

- Proverbs 31:10 – An excellent wife, who can find? For her worth is far above jewels (NASB, 861).

_____

_____

_____

_____

- 1 Peter 3:1 – In the same way, you wives, be submissive to your own husbands so that even if any of them are disobedient to the word, they may be won without a word by the behavior of their wives (NASB, 1553).

_____

_____

_____

_____

- Ephesians 5:23 – For the husband is the head of the wife, as Christ also is the head of the church, He Himself being the Savior of the body (NASB, 1519).

_____

_____

_____

_____

THINKING POINT: *How would you describe yourself as a woman, and as a wife?* Sometimes it's best to ask someone else this question about ourselves. Most often, we don't see ourselves as others do – we feel if we say good things about ourselves that we are being boastful, or arrogant. We can't help it because it's part of our Christian background.

THINKING POINT: *Where do you feel you struggle in the ministry?*

I found that ninety percent of our time spent in the ministry was a complete joy, and I felt a wonderful sense of contentment. However, there were occasions that I found cause to really struggle with people, situations, and the church as a whole. If one more person asked me why I didn't play the piano, I thought I would scream – playing the piano is not a prerequisite for being a pastor's wife! Also, I am a better follower than I am a leader. But, I was expected to be the president of the Wives' Group at church. I held that position for five years, and was internally stressed, and unhappy doing it. With maturity, I have become better equipped to handle leadership roles, but at the age of twenty-five, I floundered in trying to be something I was not. I say that my hardest struggle was to accept the lack of commitment from many in the church (you know – it's the same in your church – a <u>few</u> do <u>most</u>).

THINKING POINT: *What expectations of you as the Pastor's wife are real, and which are imagined?*

It's important for you to: (1.) make a list of those things that you believe the church, and its members expect of you. Don't hold back!!! Just brainstorm and write anything that comes into your mind. (2.) Now, go through your list, and separate those things which are truly expected, and those things which you believe are expected. You may even want to include your husband in this part of the exercise. It really is amazing to find that many of the items listed will be "imagined" expectations.

THINKING POINT: *Have you ever thought about talking to the women of your church, and explaining how you feel?*

I can hear the conversation now! Are you nuts??? I have been accused of that on some occasions. It's just a question – I never did this when Joel was pastoring in New Cumberland. I probably wouldn't have considered it at all during the first five years. However, by that point in Joel's ministry, we had developed a very strong relationship with our congregation, and I believe my thoughts and feelings would have been well received. It's at least something to consider, and ponder!

THINKING POINT: *What would you desire the church to believe about you?*

I know what I would say, Kay lives her faith, Kay loves the Lord, Kay loves her husband, and her children, Kay is a good mother, and Kay has brought people into a knowledge of, and a relationship with Jesus Christ. That is the "essence" of the life of a Christian – that's what you are, first and foremost! That's what is required of you – being a pastor's wife is secondary.

Daily Journal – This week I would like you to take the time to consider why you think God chose you to be the wife of a pastor. What qualities do you possess that God knew could be used to further His earthly kingdom? Each day write about a different aspect of your life and personality that can be used to positively impact the ministry where you are.

MONDAY

TUESDAY

WEDNESDAY

THURSDAY

FRIDAY

SATURDAY

SUNDAY

PK's –
The Perfection Game

Chapter Five

Using

Exodus 6:1-3; Deuteronomy 6:5-9; Proverbs 22:6; Ephesians 6:1-3: and Colossians 3:2—21

Chapter Five

PK's – The Perfection Game

S oon after Joel and I became engaged, one of the popular songs of 1969 was on the radio by Dusty Springfield, "Son of a Preacher Man". You may want to look up the lyrics if you are not a member of the 60's generation. This became one of "our" songs, and we often laughed about Joel being the son of a "preacher man", and the connotation that came with being a preacher's son. These boys were supposedly the bad boys girls wanted to date. They weren't too far from the truth!

Joel was raised in a parsonage until the age of eight. Christmas Day of 1955, his father died unexpectedly from a heart attack. The family was in turmoil as to where they would move after his death. Joel's mother felt the best option would be to move back to Hagerstown, Maryland, to be closer to the extended family. However, the children loved living in Westminster, and took it upon themselves to locate a place where they could live, and remain in Westminster. God directed the two oldest children to a very afford-able location, and their mother honored their wishes – she always put her children first.

The only negative issue with staying in Westminster was that Joel was to be labeled "the preacher's kid", even though his father was no longer living. Joel often talked to me about how difficult it was for him to live with that label. (I don't know if he ever shared this with his brother, or sisters, so this might surprise them.) There were times he was teased, and many times felt isolated, and treated differently by his classmates. They would change the subject when he was around, and would make comments such as, "Oh, we can't say that – Joel's a preacher's kid". He was determined to show them that he was part of the group. The pressure he felt to fit in was hard for him to handle. It caused a lot of inner conflict. The love he felt for God, and the respect he had for his mother, was totally contradictory to some of his actions. The need to belong, and fit in, is extremely strong when you are a teenager. I am convinced that it was his family's strong bond, and love for God, that helped carry Joel through these rough years.

When Joel and I arrived in New Cumberland to begin our ministry, we brought with us a two-month-old little girl named Kelly. I was instantly gifted with a huge number of people willing to babysit! Kelly was a hit from the very minute we set foot in the parsonage, and church. The congregation loved to watch her as she lay on the pew, and would raise her head up to peer over the armrest. From that moment on she was nicknamed, "Turtle". It seemed as though every move she made was a topic of conversation, and she thrived on the attention. She was the "Pastor's Daughter". At that point it was fun to hear the people talking about each sound, or new accomplishment. She was the precious, baby girl.

As each Cocklin child was born, they also found a central place in the universe of the church. The members of the congregation circled around our family, and it was wonderful. The children continued to grow, and thrive in the church environment. I'm not sure when it started to become stressful – there was no particular moment that I can associate with worrying over their behavior – it just happened.

I found myself fussing over the girls, and making sure that they were always dressed appropriately, had clean faces and hands, and I made sure to remind them that they needed to be on their best behavior. Kelly and Kim were not the ones I had to worry about. Nathan was another story! Those reading this chapter who remember our days in New Cumberland will know exactly what I'm talking about. Our son was highly energetic, and unpredictable. I was never quite sure what he would say or do.

My most embarrassing moment happened the Christmas Eve that Nathan was three. The church was packed for the Candlelight Service, and Joel had called the children forward for the "Birthday Cake for Jesus". He had completed the message for the younger ones, and asked them to return to their parents. Our children were seated in the congregation with an older couple, whom they fondly referred to as Grandma and Pop Pop (Jennie and Blaine Zimmerman). The girls started back to their seats, but Nathan looked at his daddy and said, "No, I want to stay with you!" Have you ever tried to reason with a three-year-old in front of a crowd of people? It doesn't work. He picked Nathan up, and handed him to me – I was in the Choir loft, and we were ready to sing the Christmas Eve anthem. I just looked at Joel, but what can you say in front of a packed church? I stood him down in front of me, and told him to stay there until "mommy" finished singing.

The choir began to sing, and I saw Nathan go down on all fours, crawl through the feet of the altos, back through the feet of the basses, to the edge of the row that looked down into the area where the organist was playing. The WHOLE congregation could see the pastor's son kneeling by the head of the organist, who was trying to concentrate on her music. My face was red – my husband was embarrassed – and our son was having the time of his life!

My ability to enjoy the Candlelight Service came to an abrupt end. All I could think of was how our son had disrupted the solemnity of the evening. Most people were gracious, and tried to lighten the mood, but there were those few that commented about our lack of control over our son. And we were given many suggestions as to what we should do in the future so it would never happen again. I just wanted to go home – my stomach was in a knot, and all thoughts of the blessedness of the evening were long gone.

I found many times that I worried about how my children were behaving in Sunday school, or Junior Church. Were they doing anything that Joel would hear about on Monday? I dreaded hearing the comment – "They're pastor's children. They need to set an example." We had avoided placing that burden on them. Joel remembered what it was like, and he wanted to spare them the same pressure.

When the children were six, eight, and ten years old, Joel entered the Army as a Chaplain. The biggest change we found was the lack of pressure on Chaplains' children that we had found in the local congregation. I'm not sure what it would have been like to raise teenagers in the church. My feeling is that it would have been more stressful.

I don't want you to misunderstand, and take from this that our church as a whole was responsible for my feelings of stress in this area. We were blessed with a very loving congregation. It only takes one or two critical people to create a feeling of uneasiness. One comment is all that is necessary to make you feel like you're walking on eggs every time your children are with you at a church function.

That being said, how can you combat the tension that can arise when your children create an embarrassing situation? Let me suggest several ideas:

- Make sure you have your Armor on! Especially the Belt of Truth and the Shield of Faith.

- Remind yourself that they are CHILDREN. They will not react as adults do in many situations.

- Surround yourself with other ministry wives for support.

- Find reassurance from your spouse.

- Talk to God – He's the only One whose opinion matters!

A Look at Scripture

We have already talked about the expectations that are placed on the Pastor's spouse - the only requirements that actually exist are the ones that all members need to fulfill. The same is true for your children. All children of the church should be expected to show the fruits of the Spirit as they grow. Nothing more should be required of the children of the Pastor. The Bible is very clear when giving the roadmap for developing "fruit-filled" children.

Let's look at several different passages that deal with the subject of training children. The first time God gives instruction concerning the behavior of a child is found in Exodus 20:12, the fifth commandment: "Honor your father and mother, that your days may be prolonged in the land which the Lord your God gives you." How many times did I listen to my children recite the Ten Commandments for Sunday school programs? I remember one Sunday afternoon listening to my daughter, Kim, who was seven years old. She was in her bedroom for "rest time", and apparently, they had been discussing the commandments in her class. She had her dolls lined up, and was teaching her heart out. I heard her start through the list of the commandments, and she was doing great until number seven. She hesitated, and then said in her best Sunday school teacher voice, "And thou shalt not....thou shalt not...pause, pause, pause...thou shalt not omit adultery!" I had to walk away from her door so she would not hear my hysterical laughing. Oh my! If her teacher could hear her translation of the lesson! But, all joking aside, Kimberly was learning what God expected of her. It was a beginning of her walk with her Heavenly Father, and the planting of seeds in her heart to produce good fruit in its time.

Proverbs 22:6 has been proven to be true over and over throughout the years as I have watched my children, and others struggle through those tumultuous years from age fifteen until maturity – and that can take the rest of their lives for some. The wisdom of this verse can encourage parents when it's hard to believe that their child will ever display the lessons they were raised with as Truth. The writer says, "Train up a child in the way he should go, even when he is old he will not depart from it" (NASB, 848). Your responsibility as the parent is to provide the environment for God's training to take root, and each parent prays that their child will come to the full understanding of His love for them, and the need to live according to His plan.

But how do you know what to teach them? The Israelites knew what God told them concerning training of their children. In the Pentateuch, the first five books of the Old Testament, we read in Deuteronomy 6:5-9:

> You shall love the Lord you God with all your heart and with all your soul and with all your might. These words, which I am commanding you today, shall be on your heart. You shall teach them diligently to your sons and shall talk of them when you sit in your house and when you walk by the way and when you lie down and when you rise up. You shall bind them as a sign on your hand and they shall be as frontals on your forehead. You shall write them on the doorposts of your house and on your gates (NASB, 241).

The Israelites have a name for these verses from Deuteronomy – the Shema 6. Jesus referred to this section of the Old Testament scripture when asked by a lawyer, in the book of Luke, what he needed to do to inherit eternal life. Jesus responded to him with the words from verse 5, and added two more requirements: to love God with not only your heart, soul, and strength, but also with your mind; He also told the lawyer that he must love his neighbor as himself. (Luke 10:25-27) Every parent should be clear about what God determines to be most important when instructing their children about life. If children learn these words from the Holy Scripture, chances are they will begin to display positive behavior to those around them.

My children always loved the next passage of scripture. They would get this glimmer in their eyes when the verses were read – especially if their father was preaching on this text. Colossians 3:20-21 says, "Children, be obedient to your parents in all things, for this is well-pleasing to the Lord. *Fathers, do not exasperate your children, so that they will not lose heart* [emphasis added]" (NASB, 1529). Our three always liked to use verse 21 as an excuse for their actions or attitude. It became a joke in the family, but the verse definitely rings true. If your children have behaviors that you don't like, a question you might want to ask yourself would center on those thirteen words. Is there anything I am doing that is causing my child

to be argumentative or disrespectful? We must check ourselves and

our attitudes before pointing the finger at our sons and daughters.

THINKING POINT: *How have you responded to your children*

when they have acted inappropriately in front of members of your

congregation?

If you take nothing else from this chapter, I pray that you will

understand the importance of allowing your children to make the

same mistakes the children of the congregation make. It is impor-

tant to avoid adding the pressure of being different from the rest.

Unfortunately, when your children reach a certain age, there will

be other people who will remind them that they are expected to be

models of perfect behavior, displaying all of the fruits of the Spirit.

Reassure them that this is inaccurate information. The truth is that

all of us are required as children of God, and Christians to behave

exactly the same – the standards are identical. Share with them that we all make mistakes and God is the One who we need to look to for acceptance.

THINKING POINT: *How will you know if your child/children are experiencing undue pressure from being a "preacher's kid", and possibly participating in behaviors to prove they're not different?*

I want to share with you a list of cues that can indicate that your child/children may be under stress or outside pressure. These cues were developed by the Walter Reed Army Institute of Research:

Cues Children Might Need Help

Look for changes in the child's normal behaviors and problems that persist:

*Irritability and problems controlling his/her temper

*Getting into fights, hitting, biting, and/or kicking

*Having problems paying attention or sitting still

*Withdrawing from friends and becoming a loner at school or home

*Being unhappy, sad or depressed

*Academic problems

*School personnel, friends, or others tell you that your child needs help

*Physical problems: recurrent headaches, stomachaches or unexplained fevers

(Walter Reed Army Institute of Research)

One of the best ways to make sure that you keep the lines of communication open with your children is to start early in talking openly about living in a "fish bowl". If your children feel loved and accepted by you, and understand that you are willing, and available to talk about issues of the inflated behavior expectations from members of the congregation, most of the battle is won.

The biggest stumbling block in the area of raising a preacher's kid is ignoring what might be going on inside your child. Ignoring the issue will not make it go away – it will only become bigger and harder to deal with later.

Daily Journal – Share your thoughts and experiences here on raising your children as part of a Pastor's family.

MONDAY
TUESDAY
WEDNESDAY
THURSDAY

FRIDAY

SATURDAY

SUNDAY

Parsonage Life – A Reality Show

Chapter Six

Using

Luke 7:24-27; Mark 4:35-41; Luke 10:38; and Luke 15:11-32

Chapter Six

Parsonage Life – A Reality Show

I have many memories of living in our first and only parsonage. The first memory is feeling unbelievably privileged to be moving into such a gorgeous home. Our new address was to be 507 Eutaw Avenue, New Cumberland, Pennsylvania. It was a beautiful ranch-style home with three bedrooms, and a huge family room. There was a full basement, and a detached garage. You must understand that Joel and I had just moved from a one-bedroom apartment after graduating from seminary. This home seemed like a mansion to us.

We had absolutely no furniture to add to this immense space, and had no money to purchase even one chair for the living room.

That's when our church secretary stepped in, and assisted us in locating furniture at almost no cost – second-hand furniture, but it was incredible to us! Slowly, but surely, it began to be our home.

One advantage to the parsonage was that it was not located directly beside the church. There were times that I wished it had been, so I could just run next door quickly, and then go back home. The four blocks that separated the church from our home allowed for privacy, and an opportunity to get away from the pressures of the job.

There were many funny incidents that kept life interesting on Eutaw Avenue. Soon after moving into the parsonage, we noticed that there were several female teens from the church that frequented the neighborhood. One summer evening the doorbell rang, and there were two of our female youth standing there (no names are given to protect the innocent). One of the girls was in tears, while the other did her best to console the first. We invited the girls in, and tried to figure out why the one young teen was hysterical. After much coaxing, they admitted that they had been spying on Joel by crouching in the bushes, and one of them had leaned against a burr bush, and had burrs in her long hair clear to the scalp! She just knew her mother would "kill her", and that her head would have to be shaved! I calmed her down, and asked her to let me see what I could do. I spent several hours meticulously removing each hair from the burrs. The mission was successful, and no heads had to be shaved. I believe it was that situation that allowed us to develop a strong relationship with those two girls that has endured for thirty years.

Another memorable moment came when Kelly was almost two years old, and I was pregnant with Kimberly. I had just stepped outside the front door to get the mail, but that was all it took for Kelly to shut the front door, and lock me out. Panic mode took over. No amount of pleading could get Kelly to open the door, and let me back in. My mind went into a tailspin imagining what a two year old could do alone inside the house! I ran next door to my neighbor, explained the situation (in which I found no humor), and asked to used the phone to call Joel at the church. Of course, the line was busy. I tried several times, and repeatedly heard the busy signal. In desperation, I called the operator and asked her to please interrupt the call, and put me through. She calmly said that she was only allowed to interrupt a phone conversation if it was an emergency situation. After I told her about a toddler in the house alone, and all doors locked, she immediately put me through to my husband. As Joel pulled up out front to unlock the door, we could see Kelly at the front window smiling and waving – she was having a grand ole time!

We certainly experienced many other exciting times in the parsonage – Joel being stung by bees, and having to be rushed to the ER for a shot of Adrenalin; Nathan drinking wood preservative, and going to the ER; Kim's elbow being dislocated, and going to the ER; Kelly putting a raisin up her nose, and calling the pediatrician's nurse; are you getting the picture here?? But, there were fun times, too. Each of our children was an infant in this home. We planted our first garden in this yard, and enjoyed the fruits of our labors. There were many snowy evenings by the living room fireplace, all snuggled together, while I read a story. We have many memories of that home.

There were those people that truly believed that we had an altar in our home! Imagine their amazement to discover that we had a typical home filled with children's toys, and normal decorations. We were in possession of a dog, and at various times, baby bunnies. The pastor's home is just that – a home.

Biblical Examples of a Home

Lazarus, Mary, and Martha must have had a well-run, peaceful home. Scripture doesn't tell us much about their circumstances, but it is obvious that Jesus found their home to be a place to re-group and relax. We read many times about His presence at the home of Mary and Martha. Their home was open to Jesus and the disciples, and the two women proved to be wonderful hostesses. We read nothing about the two women having a husband, or children – therefore, it would have been easy for them to entertain frequently.

What aspects of this scenario can be applied to our own home? As I read the verses that are written about Jesus' visits to the home of Lazarus, Mary, and Martha, there are four things that can be applied to our home to make it a place where the family and others want to be:

1. a strong foundation

2. an environment of peace

3. a welcoming spirit

4. a circle of love

Every building begins with the same starting point – the foundation. Several things need to be considered before beginning to place the foundation of any structure: the type of land structure, and content; the building materials; and the builder. If any of the above is of inferior quality, then the building will not be sturdy, and survive the test of time and weather. The home (a house containing a family) also requires careful planning in its construction. It needs a good foundation, exceptional materials, and a qualified builder.

But how can we create an environment of "peace" when there is no silence? There is never a quiet moment in a home when children are present. The answer rests in you. As the parent, you bring the feeling of peace to the environment. There is an amazing picture of a lighthouse in the midst of raging water. On the side of the lighthouse, facing the viewer, stands the lighthouse keeper. He is protected from the storm, and is standing in perfect peace, even with the pounding waves on all of the other sides of the building ("Phares dans le Tempete, la Jument" by Jean Guihard). We can create that same peace amid chaos by choosing to stand next to our "lighthouse in the storm" – Jesus Christ. Don't get me wrong. This is not easy. It's is impossible to accomplish peace in the middle of noise on our own. Your children and husband will be blessed beyond all measure if you can practice the presence of peace amid chaos, as only Christ can give.

Number three was very difficult for me. I desired very much to be the place where friends gathered to sit down with a cup of coffee. I never accomplished this well in the pastorate, and still struggle to throw open the doors with a "welcoming spirit." It was extremely difficult to stop stressing over "the mess!" My perceived notion that my house needed to be perfect (which it never was) kept me from inviting my friends in. I so envied a friend of mine in New Cumberland who had this gift of a welcoming spirit. To this day her door is never shut, and the door bell rings constantly with someone just stopping by to say hello, or drink a cup of coffee. Not only does she offer the hospitality of her home, and a cup of coffee, but many times the visits often bring a need for some sort of assistance. Very rarely does this woman turn down an opportunity to reach out to whoever needs her help. She has definitely succeeded in creating an environment of welcome in her home.

The fourth ingredient of the home is the most important. If you can accomplish neither peace, nor a welcoming environment, there must be love found inside the four walls of your home. Along with that love is an unconditional acceptance extended to each one who lives within those four walls. Many children and marriages have been saved through this expression of unconditional love. We turn to Jesus to observe the perfect example of this kind of love. Again, it is only through the strength that comes from Him that allows us to achieve this gift of unmerited love.

A Look at Scripture

1. A strong foundation: Luke 7:24-27 – The Wise and Foolish Builders

Therefore everyone who hears these words of mine and puts them into practice is like a wise man who built his house on the rock. The rain came down, the streams rose, and the winds blew and beat against that house; yet it did not fall, because it had its foundation on the rock. But everyone who hears these words of mine and does not put them into practice is like a foolish man who built his house on sand. The rain came down, the streams rose, and the winds blew and beat against that house, and it fell with a great crash" (NIV, 1682-1683).

As you read these four verses of Luke, I want you to think about the three stages of building the house: land, materials, and builder. In the verses, there is only one house that could withstand the falling rain (signifying troubles). The home built on solid ground, with sturdy materials, and by a master builder was able to stand against the storm.

<u>THINKING POINT</u>: *The builder is obviously Jesus. The solid ground is His word. And the sturdy materials are His Church.* Where does your home find its stability? Is your foundation grounded in Jesus, the Bible, and the Church?

2.   Peace in the midst of Chaos: Mark 4:35-41 – Jesus Calms the Storm

That day when evening came, he said to his disciples, "Let us go over to the other side." Leaving the crowd behind, they took him along, just as he was, in the boat. There were also other boats with him. A furious squall came up, and the waves broke over the boat, so that it was nearly swamped. Jesus was in the stern, sleeping on a cushion. The disciples woke him and said to him, "Teacher, don't you care if we drown?" He got up, rebuked the wind and said to the waves, "Quiet! Be still!" Then the wind died down and it was completely calm. He said to his disciples, "Why are you so afraid? Do you still have no faith?" They were terrified and asked each other, "Who is this? Even the wind and the waves obey him" (NIV, 1633).

Mark shares a story with us that is the perfect example of peace amid chaos!

Read these verses, and in place of a boat use the words "my house". And instead of the words "A furious squall came up" use "a lot of loud, screaming voices". The story takes on a new meaning for every mother. Chaos has erupted in your house – have you ever referred to your children as "howler monkeys"? This is the scene that I want you to imagine. Then view Jesus peacefully asleep on your couch, and you wonder, "How can He be sound asleep with all of this craziness around Him?" And Jesus will tell you the same thing He told His disciples, "Why are you so stressed (afraid)?"

THINKING POINT: *Can you see the parallel between the experience of the disciples on the boat in the midst of the storm, and the chaos that can reign frequently in the home? How peaceful can you remain during these times? Remember: You're not alone in the "boat"!!!*

3. A Welcoming Spirit: Luke 10:38 – At the Home of Martha and Mary

As Jesus and his disciples were on their way, he came to a village where a woman named Martha opened her home to him" (NIV, 1689).

Such a simple verse, but it has such a powerful message: "As Jesus and his disciples were on their way, he came to a village where a woman named Martha opened her home to him." WOW! To me those few words speak volumes! Can you imagine if a very famous preacher – maybe Billy Graham – was traveling through your hometown? With no previous notification of his arrival, would you open your door, and invite him in? OR, would you hesitate because your house was not completely straight? Maybe there were toys from one end of the house to the other (often the case in my home), and possibly there was laundry to be folded lying on the couch. And in that hesitation, you missed an opportunity to welcome the honored preacher into your home for a time of rest and refreshment. It's taken me a long time to realize that most people come to see me, not to see whether my house is ready for <u>Better Homes and Gardens</u>.

<u>THINKING POINT</u>: *It's important to recognize that when we open our homes to others that we open the opportunity to share Christ with those who enter. When I keep the focus on this possibility, then I find that it is easier to ignore the "mess", and enjoy the company.*

1. A Circle of Love: Luke 15:11-32 – The Parable of the Lost Son

Jesus continued: "There was a man who had two sons. The younger one said to his father, 'Father, give me my share of the estate.' So he divided his property between them. Not long after that, the younger son got together all he had, set off for a distant country and there squandered his wealth in wild living. After he had spent everything, there was a severe famine in that whole country, and he began to be in need. So he went and hired himself out to a citizen of that country, who sent him to his fields to feed pigs. He longed to fill his stomach with the pods that the pigs were eating, but no one gave him anything. When he came to his senses, he said, 'How many of my father's hired men have food to spare, and here I am starving to death! I will set out and go back to my father and say to him: Father, I have sinned against heaven and against you. I am no longer worthy to be called your son; make me like one of your hired men.' So he got up and went to his father. But while he was still a long way off, his father saw him and was filled with compassion for him; he ran to his son, threw his arms around him and kissed him. The son said to him, 'Father, I have sinned against heaven and against you. I am no longer worthy to be called your son. But the father said to his servants, 'Quick! Bring the best robe and put it on him. Put a ring on his finger and sandals on his feet. Bring the fattened calf and kill it. Let's have a feast and celebrate. For this son of mine was dead and is alive again; he was lost and is found.' So they began to celebrate. Meanwhile, the older son was in the field. When he came near the house, he heard music and dancing. So he called one of the servants and asked him what was going on. 'Your brother has come,' he replied, 'and your father has killed the fattened calf because he has him back safe and sound.' The older brother became angry and refused to go in. So his father went out and pleaded with him. But he answered his father, 'Look! All these years I've been slaving for you and never disobeyed your orders. Yet you never gave me even a young goat so I could celebrate with my friends. But when this son of yours who has squandered your property with prostitutes comes home, you kill the fattened calf for him!' 'My son,' the father said, 'you are always with me, and everything I have is yours. But we had to celebrate and be glad, because this brother of yours was dead and is alive again; he was lost and is found' (NIV, 1698-1700).

One of the great "love" messages in the Bible is found in this chapter. Can you imagine giving your child a large sum of money, his/her inheritance, and allowing the child to leave the security of home to venture out into the world? And then this child foolishly squanders every bit of the money, participates in unmentionable activities, only to return home when there is no other choice? The father in Luke 15, reacted with unconditional love, AND, the scripture says that he was watching for the child's return – an unending vigil of prayer, petition, and longing on the part of the father.

THINKING POINT*: How would you react? Can you honestly say that you would run to meet your child, cover him with an expensive robe, and have a feast in his honor??? And, no mention of "I told you so"!*

Daily Journal – Write about how the pressures of the ministry have affected your child. In what ways can you help to alleviate some of the negative aspects of being a "preacher's kid".

MONDAY

TUESDAY

WEDNESDAY

THURSDAY

FRIDAY

SATURDAY

SUNDAY

Finding Your "Nitch", Instead of a Rut or a Hole!

Chapter Seven

Using

Various Old and New Testament Scripture

Chapter Seven

Finding Your "Nitch"
Instead of a Rut or Hole!

E ach woman, as she enters the ministry with her husband, must start at the beginning – and as Fraulein Maria said to her charges in "The Sound of Music" – it's a very good place to start! As a pastor's wife, I had to find my "nitch" in the church. A nitch is a small location, or mark in a large area. Where was I to fit into Joel's ministry in New Cumberland? There were many people who gave me unsolicited advice: I could play the piano; I could be President of WCSC; I could teach Sunday school; I could sing in the choir; and the list went on and on. But, the question remained –

What did I want to do? AND, what was I capable of doing?

The mistake I see so many wives make is jumping in with both feet, and committing themselves to too many facets of the church. This "nitch finding" should be a slow process, because each church is different. What you may have done in one church may not transfer to another church. My first bit of advice is to take your time, and get to know the particular ministries of the church.

The second mistake I have witnessed is not taking into consideration the gifts you possess. I discovered that just because something sounded fun didn't necessarily mean I should be the one in charge of the activity. It is vitally important to make an assessment of your specific gifts, and there are many tools available to assist you in locating areas of ministry where you will be most effective. Also, ask trusted friends what they have seen in your life that would be considered a gift. Remember: *Whatever you are passionate about is most likely where you will find your gift from God.* He plants in us special interests and desires, and those will point the way to where we should serve in ministry.

The third trap on your journey of finding your nitch is the "people-pleasing" trap. Some of us are just naturally people-pleasers! We worry constantly if someone is unhappy with us, or if we feel we have disappointed someone. As a young pastor's wife I was easily persuaded to take on responsibilities that were not in my area of "giftedness". At first, I was honored to be asked to assume certain roles in our new church. At other times, I was reluctant to say no because I felt it would look bad on my part, and that it indicated that I was not supportive of the church. So, instead of finding my nitch, I found a "rut"!!! I soon discovered that it is extremely difficult to climb out of a rut. Unfortunately, after trying unsuccessfully to dig your way out of a rut, you find that you are now in a hole! You can only find your way out of a hole with assistance. No one can get out of a hole by themselves.

What we must realize though is that there are times that God will remove us from our comfort zone, and ask us to serve Him in areas that can cause anxiety, and discomfort. There are many instances in scripture where God called men and women to leave their place of giftedness. There is a very fine line here that requires prayerful discernment. The call of God, and the call of "Man" can sound very similar. Often we use the words of people as validation that God wants us to do certain things. Tread carefully here. It is very easy to misinterpret, and then respond incorrectly. This is a time for the use of God's Armor. At this moment you will need verse 14, and verse 18 of Ephesians 6: you will need the belt of Truth, and the prayers of the Spirit. The call to service in the church should never be taken lightly, and without a season of prayer.

Two Examples of Men Called Out of Their Comfort Zone

As we read the book of Exodus, we discover the story of Moses. Throughout chapters two and three, we see several traits of Moses that we would definitely consider to be strengths, or gifts. Exodus 2: 1-10 tells us about his birth, his mother's sacrifice, and the rescue by the Pharaoh's daughter. After Moses had grown older, the daughter of the Pharaoh claimed him as her son. He must have displayed qualities during his early years that proved that he was worthy of being called the "grandson" of the ruler. As a young adult, Moses recognized the cruelty of the treatment being forced upon the Israelites, and retaliated for his native people. Moses displayed his leadership gifts as a young man. But, as we read chapter three, God calls Moses to greater responsibility, and his reaction was to come up with several excuses for the Lord. Have you ever used any of these?

1. "Who am I, that I should go to Pharaoh and bring back the Israelites out of Egypt?" (Ch 3, vs.11)

2. "Suppose I go to the Israelites and say to them, 'The God of your fathers has sent me to you.' And they ask me, 'What is his name?' Then what shall I tell them?" (Ch 3, vs. 13)

3. "What if they do not believe me or listen to me and say, 'The Lord did not appear to you'?" (Ch.4, vs. 1)

4. "O Lord, I have never been eloquent, neither in the past nor since you have spoken to your servant. I am slow of speech and tongue." (Ch 4, vs. 10)

5. "O Lord, *please send someone else to do it* [emphasis
   added]." (Ch 4, vs. 13)

Moses was definitely out of his comfort zone in this mission
that God had called him to carry out. But the Lord did not let up
on Moses until he agreed to answer the call to rescue the people of
Israel, and bring them out of bondage.

The second person pulled out of his comfort zone was Jonah!
Jonah didn't even bother with any excuses for God – he most likely
realized that God wouldn't listen to his excuses anyway! Jonah just
ran away. Psalm 139 explains very clearly to each of us that there
is no place that will hide us from the eyes of God. "Where can I
go from your Spirit? Where can I flee from your presence? If I go
up to the heavens, you are there; if I make my bed in the depths,
you are there" (NIV, 574). After running from God unsuccessfully,
Jonah offers no excuses. He submitted to the call to bring salvation
to the Ninevites. Jonah, as we know, was not happy that God actually saved the people of Nineveh, but that is a whole other story!

Those Who Served According to Their Gift

Read the following scripture passages that describe how Old and New Testament men and women used their gifts to further the kingdom of God on earth.

PERSON	SCRIPTURE	GIFT
David	1 Samuel 16:1-13	Leadership
Ruth	Ruth 1:16-18	Steadfastness; love
Job	The Book of Job	Perseverance
Jeremiah	Jeremiah 1:5	Prophecy
John the Baptist	Matthew 3:1-16	Evangelism
Solomon	I Kings 3:16-28	Wisdom
The Roman Centurion	Matthew 8:1-13	Faith
Mary	Luke 1:26-38	Obedience
Paul	All of Paul's writing in the New Testament	Teaching

Your Turn

YOUR NAME	YOUR GIFT/GIFTS

THINKING POINT: *Why is it that so often we envy those who have gifts that we don't? How many times do we say to ourselves, "If only I had (...........) gift, then I would really be able to participate in volunteering my time at the church"? Why can't we be satisfied with what God has granted to us as His gift to be used in His creation?*

There were so many times that I envied my sister's talent on the piano. Playing seemed to come so easily to her – no composition was too difficult. My parents loved to listen to her play, and would always ask her to perform in front of guests in our home. How I longed to have her skill on the "ebonies and ivories"! My gifting was in art – I could draw whatever I saw. But, who cared about that? I was never asked to perform before guests in the house. My gift of drawing was not in the least bit comparable to my sister's gift of music. Interestingly enough, I discovered many years later that my sister wanted my gift!! We're never satisfied!

THINKING POINT: *Are you using the gifts God gave you to edify the church?* You've heard the saying, "Use it, or lose it!" In Matthew 25:14-30, Christ preached about that long before the saying – it may well have come from this verse. In verse 28 and 29, we are warned, "Take the talent from him and give it to the one who has the ten talents. For everyone who has will be given more, and he will have abundance. Whoever does not have, even what he has will be taken from him" (NASB, 1282). God expects us to make use of the gifts we are given to multiply the harvest. When we ignore the talents that are freely given to us, those talents will be taken away.

THINKING POINT: *How can you graciously refuse to participate in activities of the church that do not fall in the area of your "gift-edness"?* This is still difficult for me to do. It can definitely be an uncomfortable situation when you are asked to consider filling a role that you know you shouldn't. Some people do not want to accept the idea that you have the right to say no. It's possible that you don't realize that you have that right! Practice saying "no". Start with little things, and work your way up to the big requests. You can do it – you may always feel a little twinge of guilt each time, but you must be prayerful that God will allow the right person to be guided into the position. Have you ever thought that by saying yes to every request, you may be denying someone the chance to use their gift? You must consider that possibility.

Daily Journal – *Reminisce about times when you have answered yes, and it's been a disaster. Then write about times when you know you have found your nitch and wonderful things happened. Lastly, write about times that God has called you out of your comfort zone to accomplish things for Him.*

SUNDAY

MONDAY

TUESDAY

WEDNESDAY

THURSDAY

FRIDAY

SATURDAY

The "Two-for-One" Misconception

Chapter Eight

Using

1 Corinthians 12:12-30

Chapter Eight

The Two-for-One Misconception

Everyone loves a bargain! I love to shop during the week when you can redeem coupons, or when Kohl's has a 60% off sale! It's the mind-set of getting "something for nothing". It is possible for the church to look at the new pastor, and his wife in that same light. The old "two-for-one" concept creeps into the mindset of the congregation. Occasionally, pastors have been known to perpetuate this belief themselves. What do we do when faced with a church that believes they have just hired two pastors, but are only paying for one?

Let there be no misunderstanding - unless both the husband and wife have been ordained by the conference, and the contract includes both names, there is only one person that is required to fulfill the guidelines of the contract. The spouse must see her role in the light of any other member of the church, and no more. It is the responsibility of the pastor to clearly state that his spouse in under no more obligation to serve the church than any other member of the congregation. When a church understands this fact, then the wife can feel free to join in those activities that God calls her to do.

We must be very careful as wives to avoid usurping the position of our husband. Over the years I have observed situations that were not healthy in the ministry. Also, I experienced first-hand the results of being too prominent in the ministry of my husband. I have the gift of teaching. It is my passion to instruct children, and watch the learning that takes place in each one. While Joel served in Heidelberg, Germany, I was responsible for the Children's Sermon on Sunday mornings. It was pure joy to sit at the front of the Chapel, and explain the wonders of God to those little eager ears. What became abundantly clear was that I created a situation that affected the role of my husband. Comments were made to Joel that the

Children's Sermon was easier to understand than the adult sermon, and that maybe I could preach from the pulpit some time! I'm sure that the comments were given lightheartedly, but they hurt my husband anyway. We were not sent there to be dual Chaplains, or to be in competition with each other. It became my responsibility to discover another means to fulfill my desire to use my gift of teaching. I began volunteering in the Sunday school program, Vacation Bible School, and in the Junior Church classroom, which was away from the eyes and ears of the congregation. As wives, we are there to compliment, and support our pastor husbands, never to be in competition with them.

Your role as the Pastor's Wife is extremely important. You and your husband **ARE** a package deal! The presence of the wife is reassuring to the members of the congregation. It's always sad to see a church that experiences the non-involvement of the pastor's spouse. There seems to be a hole in the heart of the church. The following is a list of the roles correctly included in the package deal:

- Prayer Warrior

- Worship attendee

- Listening ear

- Friendly face

- Encourager

- Volunteer

- Giver of tithes and offerings

As you can see from the list, these roles would apply to any member of the church. However, your role as Pastor's Wife is a role no one else in the church can fill. It is an honored spot – some denominations even refer to the wife as the "First Lady", and she always sits on the front pew.

It is always difficult to follow in the footsteps of a pastor who was extremely loved by the church. Equally so, it is hard to follow behind a Pastor's Wife who has been the "end-all and be-all" of the church. The church experiences a period of adjustment to the new wife, who may not be as active a participant as the previous wife. One thing both you and the congregation need to realize is that you can never be that other person. You are unique, and you bring your own personality, interests, and gifts to the church. Never feel pressured to be someone, or something that you are not. It would result in a disaster to even try.

I found that members of the congregation assume that the Pastor's wife has the same training as her husband. There were many times I was asked questions requiring deep Biblical knowledge – and I faced a "Black Hole" in my brain when searching for an answer. I soon learned to respond by saying that I did not have an answer for that specific question, but that I was sure my husband might. (A hint: Early in my husband's ministry, I responded to questions by saying that I would ask my husband, and get back to them with the answer. However, most often the answer was beyond my understanding – so, I quickly learned to refer them directly to him, and therefore removed the "middle man".)

Situations like this can create frustration, and anxiety for you as the spouse. As much as you want to help, you need to realize that you are not trained to deal with many issues. The stark realization is that your husband has been called to the ministry by God, and has received the training necessary to pastor his "flock". Make every effort to demonstrate to the congregation that he is the first-line of communication for the church members and their needs.

Our Model for Being a Member of God's Church

God had a design from the beginning for His Church, and how His family should function together perfectly. When each segment of the Church carries out its specific job, then the world sees what God is like. 1 Corinthians 12:12-30 illustrates exactly how each of us fits into the inner workings of His Church. The following was taken from the New American Standard Bible:

> For even as the body is one and yet has many members, and *all the members of the body, though they are many, are one body* [emphasis mine], so also is Christ. For by one Spirit we were all baptized into one body, whether Jews or Greeks, whether slaves or free, and we were all made to drink of one Spirit. For the body is not one member, but many. If the foot says, "Because I am not a hand, I am not a part of the body," it is not for this reason any the less a part of the body.

And if the ear says, "Because I am not an eye, I am not a part of the body," it is not for this reason any the less a part of the body. If the whole body were an eye, where would the hearing be? If the whole were hearing, where would the sense of smell be? ***But now God has placed the members, each one of them, in the body, just as He desired*** [emphasis mine]. If they were all one member, where would the body be? But now there are many members, but one body. And the eye cannot say to the hand, "I have no need of you"; or again the head to the feet, "I have no need of you." On the contrary, it is much truer that the members of the body which seem to be weaker are necessary; and those members of the body which we deem less honorable, on these we bestow more abundant honor, and our less presentable members become much more presentable, whereas our more presentable members have no need of it. But God has so composed the body, giving more abundant honor to that member which lacked, so that there may be no division in the body, but that the members may have the same care for one another. And if one member suffers, all the members suffer with it; if one member is honored, all the members rejoice with it. ***Now you are Christ's body, and individually members of it. And God has appointed in the church, first apostles, second prophets, third teachers, then miracles, then gifts of healings, helps, administrations, various kinds of tongues. All are not apostles, are they? All are not prophets, are they? All are not teachers, are they? All are not workers of miracles, are they? All do not have gifts of healings, do they? All do not speak with tongues, do they? All do not interpret, do they*** (NASB, 1488-1489 [emphasis mine]).

I have always wondered what part of the "body" of Christ I am! When I look at the gifts that God has given to me, I can determine which body parts and functions I possess. I have the gift of "listening" – so I am an ear! Caring and compassion are very important to me, and each day I find myself lending my shoulder for those experiencing difficulty – so I am a shoulder! My nickname has often been "Sunshine" because of my constant smile – so I must be a mouth, too! Encouragement to others comes easily to me, and I love to HUG – I am definitely arms! Those are my strong attributes for the body of the Church, but verse 22 talks about the presence of "weaker members", and I obviously have those, also. The scripture encourages us that even the weak parts of the body can still be used and are considered important.

It was fun to look at my strong parts, but I'm not as excited about bringing to light the areas that are not as well developed. I am aware that I have not been God's feet that are diligently going out to seek those who are lost. It's obvious that I am not His hands that reach out in service to the needy. The brain? Well, there is no question that I do not have the capacity to reveal the deep revelations of the Lord to His people. How I would love to be His knees! My mother was God's knees. I remember watching her night after night, on her knees, praying for forty-five minutes or longer. That is not my gift. But, I thank God that even though these areas are weak, He still uses the small amount that I offer. I know that I have at least brought one person to Christ; I have been of service to a small number of people throughout my life; I have used what knowledge I possess to reveal God's Truth to several groups of women; and I pray every day for those who need God's care.

The amazing part of God is that He takes each one of us, and gives us specific gifts, or talents. No one receives all of the gifts, just like no one can be the WHOLE body. It is important to remember, as you serve in your role as the Pastor's wife, that you cannot be "*every*"thing to "*every*"one! God created you with a special purpose from the very beginning – you are unique – one-of-a-kind! Each of us has the task of recognizing our strengths and our weaknesses, and then moving forward to help God's Church function in the world. It will remove the weight of the world off of your shoulders to realize that you are not expected to tackle every issue, project, need, or committee in the church. Do I hear a loud exhale; Praise the Lord, and Amen??? Because that's what I did when I came to the amazing revelation that it didn't all depend on me!

What Parts of the Body Are You?

THINKING POINT: *Take time to consider both your strong parts and your weak parts. Make a list of those and then consider where you are able to use them in your local church. Determine if the activities you are already involved in are areas using your strong parts or your weak parts. What did you discover? Is the majority of your time and talents being used in your strong or weak set of "parts"?*

Strong Part	Activity

Weak Part	Activity

What did you discover as you looked at your areas of strong and weak parts? Write an evaluation of your compared lists.

THINKING POINT: *As you look over your ministry with your hus-band so far, have there been times when you may have overshadowed him and assumed too much of the "Pastor" role in the church where you are presently serving?* I'm sure there are those who disagree with me on this point; however, there is a fine line which should be carefully followed in a husband and wife ministry team. Your husband should never be made to feel he has to compete with you in the leadership role of the church.

Your reactions

Daily Journal: *Spend a few minutes each day considering your areas of strength, and how you can use these to benefit the members of your church.*

MONDAY
TUESDAY

WEDNESDAY

THURSDAY

FRIDAY

SATURDAY

SUNDAY

Balancing the Teeter-Totter

Chapter Nine

Using

Ecclesiastes 3:1-14

Chapter Nine

Balancing the Teeter-Totter

T here are several professions that fall into the category of the "teeter-totter" balancing game. Physicians, hospital personnel, law enforcement, fire safety, funeral directors, and ministers are among those who are always on call. They are public servants who struggle with finding a balance in their lives as a professional, and as a member of a family. Unfortunately, it seems like one of the two usually suffers from lack of attention.

For the first several years of Joel's ministry, this was an area that caused a great amount of stress for both of us. Being a pastor is an extremely demanding profession. For the dedicated servant of God, there is no time that you can truly call your own unless you make a conscious decision to prioritize your life. As a new pastor, Joel was ready to set the world on fire, and breathe life into the church. He literally hit the ground running when we arrived in New Cumberland.

Joel was ordained June 23, 1972, in Elizabethtown, PA. It was during that very week that the heavens opened up, and the rain began to fall. Hurricane Agnes had situated itself right over Central Pennsylvania, and the entire area was being deluged with rain. By the time we returned to New Cumberland, half of the town was under water – thanks to the Susquehanna River. For the next two to three weeks, the New Cumberland First Church of God was "Sandwich Central"! From sunup to sundown the kitchen in the basement of the church teemed with activity. Every person in the lower half of town received food and any assistance possible during the crisis of the flood.

This time of outreach was a tremendous blessing not only for the people who lost all of their worldly possessions, but it was a blessing for Joel and me. Out of a disaster came an amazing opportunity for us to be introduced into the new church, and the community. However, it also set a pace that carried over into the months to come. The church and the community were consuming a huge portion of each twenty-four hour day. The family time was suffering, and I didn't quite know how to approach the topic without seeming critical. I knew I would come off sounding whiney!

When I finally did bring up the subject of the lack of family time, it mainly created frustration, stress, and guilt for Joel. He had been aware of the unbalanced time, but clearly had no answer as to how to make everyone happy. So, we just continued marching on, "being good soldiers", and trying to make the most of the time we did have to spend in family time.

It became obvious to me, after we added two more children to our family, that a change was necessary. The following schedule was a typical day for Joel:

- 8 AM – leave for the office
- Noon – maybe home for lunch, if there was no meeting – most often there was a meeting
- 6 PM – home for supper

- 7 PM – meeting at Church (usually Monday through Thursday)

- 10 – 11 PM – home

The children and Joel were not being able to spend any time together, and neither were we. I was becoming very desperate, and was ready for drastic measures! An idea began to form as to a possible way to spend some time with my husband, but not take away from his time at the church.

One morning, as Joel was getting ready to go to the church, I got his appointment book, and wrote my name down for a one hour counseling session. I knew that I would have his undivided attention during that one hour of time. Can you imagine his surprise when he got to work, and saw who was scheduled to see him first thing in the morning??? I kept my appointment, and we had a great laugh, and enjoyed our uninterrupted time together. Fortunately for me, I have a very smart husband, and he realized that if I had to set an appointment to see him, then there were some things that needed to change.

There are other issues in serving the church that can cause the teeter-totter to become unbalanced. As much as I fought against it, there were times I became jealous over the time my husband spent with his "other" women. Now, granted, these women had legitimate counseling sessions, and in my rational mind I understood that. Also, women were always at the church. Joel was fun to be with, and they enjoyed talking to him, and spending time in his office just passing the time of day. Putting these feelings into words so many years later just seems so petty and immature. But, they were real feelings, and needed to be dealt with through husband and wife communication. Do you understand how difficult it is to explain female emotions to the opposite sex?? And, there is no real resolution to this situation. It was my issue to deal with – my husband's job was to minister to each individual requesting his expertise. I spent much time in prayer, asking God to do what I couldn't do: Fill me with peace. That was how the teeter-totter in this area became level. When you find that you can't balance the see-saw, God will step in, and do it for you. Do you remember, as a child, trying to balance the see-saw?

Sometimes you could do it by leaning backwards or moving further back on your end. Other times you would ask someone just the right size to climb on with you, and everything leveled out. This is what God can do for you in many circumstances when you can't make things *even out*.

For me, one of the most upsetting occurrences of the ministry centered around family plans – date night, family-fun-night, dinner time, and most especially, family vacations. I soon discovered that the minute the family planned some time together, something would come along to interfere with those plans. There are a lot of parts to "Murphy's Law" that they don't tell you about! There were many times that Joel and I had to look at three disappointed faces, and explain why "Mr. or Mrs. So and So's" problem came before our fun. Children don't always understand priorities, and to be perfectly honest, I wasn't always the most gracious wife to accept the change in plans either. The teeter-totter becomes very unbalanced in these situations, and it takes real skill to bring it back to the level position. I'm sure you've heard the phrase, "Choose your battles." Likewise, the pastor needs to determine which church member needs outweigh the needs of his family. There are some situations that can wait a few hours, or days. And then there are legitimate emergencies that take precedence over family plans. Disappointments are bound to happen, but the pastor must strive to keep a healthy balance between his obligations to the church family, and the needs of his own family.

What Does God Say About Balance?

One of the best references to use with the topic of balancing time and family is found in Ecclesiastes 3:1-14.

A Time for Everything

There is an appointed time for everything. And there is a time for every event under heaven—

A time to give birth and a time to die;

A time to plant and a time to uproot what is planted.

A time to kill and a time to heal;

A time to tear down and a time to build up. A time to weep and

a time to laugh;

A time to mourn and a time to dance.

A time to throw stones and a time to gather stones;

A time to embrace and a time to shun embracing.

A time to search and a time to give up as lost;

A time to keep and a time to throw away.

A time to tear apart and a time to sew together;

A time to be silent and a time to speak.

A time to love and a time to hate;

A time for war and a time for peace.

What profit is there to the worker from that in which he toils?

I have seen the task which God has given the sons of men with

which to occupy themselves (NASB, 864).

God Set Eternity in the Heart of Man

He has made everything appropriate in its time He has also
set eternity in their heart, yet so that man will not find out
the work which God has done from the beginning even to
the end. I know that there is nothing better for them than to

rejoice and to do good in one's lifetime; moreover, that every man who eats and drinks sees good in all his labor—it is the⁾ gift of God. I know that everything God does will remain forever; there is nothing to add to it and there is nothing to take from it, for God has so worked that men should fear Him (NASB, 864-865).

Each verse in the third chapter of Ecclesiastes gives us a guideline of how God has designed our days. He created us to enjoy life, and to be in relationship with Him. The Fall of Adam and Eve changed the scheme of things. The necessity for man to work and toil was added to the schedule. Woman was to experience pain as she labored to bring life into the world. The natural balance that God intended was destroyed, and it requires us to strive to bring that balance back through our relationship with Him, with Christ, and with our family. What was planned to be easy became difficult.

THINKING POINT: *What you have just finished reading about are the areas of the ministry that kept my "teeter-totter" unbalanced occasionally. I may not even have discussed situations in your experience that have caused the see-saw to tilt. Are there times when you and your husband have had to consciously bring a more leveled*

position back into your ministry?

_____

_____

_____

_____

_____

_____

THINKING POINT: *What strategies have you used to establish a*

good balance between church and family?

_____

_____

_____

_____

_____

_____

Daily Journal: Each day take a verse from our Ecclesiastes text and focus on what God is telling you.

SUNDAY	
MONDAY	
TUESDAY	
WEDNESDAY	

THURSDAY	
FRIDAY	
SATURDAY	

BFF?? What's That?

Chapter Ten

using

1 and 2 Samuel, Ruth, and various New Testament Passages

Chapter Ten

BFF?? What's That?

With the cell phone generation, and the texting phenomenon, we have a new language that has erupted, and filters into our written conversation today. We have "LOL", which means "laugh out loud"; there is "BTW", which translates to "by the way"; and then, of course, we can't leave out "WTG", which means "way to go"! Television commercials have picked up on the texting vocabulary, and have used the acronym "BFF" quite frequently. Most living and breathing human beings understand that to mean "Best Friends Forever"! Whoa be it unto those, who do not understand the jargon of the "Y" generation. You will be left out in the cold, finding yourself alone with an outdated vocabulary.

Do you remember your first best friend?? I do. His name was Johnny Kroh. Our mothers both taught second grade at West End Primary School, in Westminster, Maryland. We spent a lot of time together at the school, and became best friends. We even decided before first grade that one day we would get married, and have a horse farm. Johnny continued to be my best friend through most of the elementary grades. We built tree houses together, went on bike hikes in the summer, and had fun sledding in the winter. Our parents even built a cabin together by the Monocacy River, where we spent glorious carefree days.

In sixth grade my new best friend was Joel Cocklin. This was the first year that we were in the same class. I remember that he was well-liked, and just plain fun to be with at school. He was at every party I had – he'd be the first person there, and the last person to leave. Our friendship continued throughout the school years, until twelfth grade, when I believe hormones kicked in (can I write that in a Christian book?), and we began dating.

Of course, I had female friends, too. Those changed throughout the years of primary school, elementary school, junior and senior high school, and then college. Each one meant something special to me throughout the years, and they fulfilled the God-given need for friendship, and the need to belong. "When we honestly ask ourselves which person in our lives means the most us, we often find that it is those who, instead of giving much advice, solutions, or cures, have chosen rather to share our pain and touch our wounds with a gentle and tender hand. The friend who can be silent with us in a moment of despair or confusion, who can stay with us in an hour of grief and bereavement, who can tolerate not knowing, not curing, not healing and face with us the reality of our powerlessness, that is a friend who cares."- Henri Nouwen

The need to belong is one of our strongest desires. This need is first met as we become part of a family unit, and we begin to find our place in that group. But, as we grow, we add to our "friend base" by forming small groups of acquaintances beyond the four walls of the home. These friendships allow us to develop healthy connections, and the ability to socialize outside of the family. The bonds that can develop between two people fills a "void" that allows human beings to become whole. "The worst solitude is to be destitute of sincere friendship," Francis Bacon.

Why are we even discussing this need to belong, and the bonds of friendship? Those of you who have been in the ministry for a short time know that it is difficult to develop a close bond with those who are members of your church. We walk a fine line as pastor's wives in many areas, and this is one of them. Being the spouse of a minister can be a very lonely life. I have spoken to quite a few wives, and each one asked me if there would be a chapter in the book devoted to the feeling of loneliness.

In a community of believers that is known for its ability to love, and extend its arms of friendship to the world, how is it possible for the pastor's wife to feel lonely? There are a number of reasons:

- When you are the wife of a pastor, you are held on a higher plane.

- Jealousy can enter into the hearts of other women that feel excluded from a bond that develops between yourself and another member.

- Women feel that they are not "good enough" to be your friend.

- You can't let down, and share everything for fear of bringing criticism on your husband.

- Due to the confidentiality issue of your husband's job, there are many things he will not be able to share with you.

Let's look at each of these reasons one at a time.

It didn't take me very long after moving to New Cumberland, and beginning our ministry there, to realize that people don't have conversations with the pastor and his wife like they do with "normal" people. Most of the dialogue always gravitated toward religious topics. I guess it's like when you meet with your doctor at social events, you talk about health related issues. I got to the point that if I met someone new, I would not tell them what my husband did for a living. An interesting situation arose during our years in New Cumberland that was quite amusing at the time, and is just down-right funny today!

Kelly had been taking ballet lessons in Camp Hill for around six months. The mothers and I had formed a close friendship, and enjoyed our time together while our daughters danced. One lesson day Joel's car was in the shop, so I had to leave to pick him up from a counseling session, and take him back to the church. I asked the other mothers to explain to Kelly, if she asked where I was, that I had gone to White Hill (a State Correctional Institution in Camp Hill, PA) to pick up her father, and that I would be right back. I noticed a look pass between the mothers, but I never thought any-more about it. When I returned there was dead silence in the room. Finally, one of the mothers looked at me, and said, "Kay, what does your husband dooooo?" I took a deep breath, and responded that I always hated when this subject came up, because once I told people, the relationship always changed. The women looked at each other, and nodded in agreement. I've never seen such focused attention as I began to explain what my husband "did" for a living. The sigh of relief that came from the women as I told them that my husband was a minister confused me. That's when one of the moms said that they had thought my husband was a prisoner at White Hill, and they didn't think they just let them out like that. We had a great laugh, and our friendship continued throughout the rest of the ballet season.

When our children were old enough to enter kindergarten I began to develop friendships that started to fulfill the need in my life for a "kindred" spirit. Our common interest in the classroom activities and in our children formed bonds that exist to this day. Finally, I didn't have to be concerned about any conflict of interest, or hurting someone else's feelings! However, as our friendships grew these new friends began attending services at the church, and many continued into membership there. I was right back where I started! Joel's guidance was to continue doing everything I had been doing with this small group of people – shopping, coffee, week-end trips, and picnics. You wouldn't think that would cause anybody any heartburn. There were a few people who expressed their criticisms about showing favoritism to some, while excluding others. This was a perfect time to realize the value of believing that you can't please everyone! I will never regret continuing to include these people in my life. They still remain some of my dearest, and most supportive Christian friends. I thank God for them every day. I would mention them, but they know who they are.

Some women in the church will not approach you because they are under the mistaken impression that you are perfect, and would never understand the problems they deal with every day. (Some even believed that we had an altar in our home!) These women are ashamed of past issues, and believe you could never have experienced making the same wrong choices in your life. It's very possible that those in the ministry have perpetuated this false front, and encouraged hiding behind masks of perfection. I was never proud of the wrong choices I had made, but I never tried to hide them either. People need to understand that "all have sinned and fall short of the glory of God" (NASB, 1461), and that pastors' wives fall into the category of "all".

After having said everything in the previous paragraph, now I have to add a footnote to subject of sharing. Unfortunately, discussing past sins does not equate with revealing our present sins to a member of the congregation. The mark of true friendship is the ability to be completely honest – to lay open your soul – to this other person. In return, each receives total acceptance and unconditional love. Along with those two expressions of friendship is also the responsibility to be completely honest about each other's faults. This model for developing friendship is definitely supported by scripture. However, this type of friendship is rarely found between the wife of the pastor, and a member of the congregation. The fact remains that a barrier will always exist that prevents complete honesty for fear of creating a stumbling block for your husband's ministry.

In this chapter we also need to look at how the confidentiality of your husband's profession can also affect the honest and open sharing between the two of you as a couple. On numerous occasions my husband would come home after a long day at work. My first questions would be, "How was your day? What did you do all day?"

More often than not, he would just say that he couldn't discuss his day because most of his time was spent in counseling sessions. It made me feel "weird" to realize others shared "secrets" with Joel that I was not allowed to know. I understand how ridiculous that sounds, but those are the feelings I experienced. So, not only was I not able to share 100% of my life with a friend, I was also not allowed to be included in 100% of my husband's life. It's difficult not to become resentful of these private moments with others.

Biblical Friendships

__David and Jonathan__: Now it came about when he had finished speaking to Saul, that the soul of Jonathan was knit to the soul of David, and Jonathan loved him as himself. (1 Samuel18:1, [NASB])

After David had finished talking with Saul, Jonathan became one in spirit with David, and he loved him as himself. From that day Saul kept David with him and did not let him return to his father's house.

And Jonathan made a covenant with David because he loved him as himself. Jonathan took off the robe he was wearing and gave it to David, along with his tunic, and even his sword, his bow and his belt. (1 Samuel 18:1-4, [NIV])

The Life Application Bible states in its commentary that David and Jonathan's friendship was "one of the deepest and closest recorded in the Bible: (1) they based their friendship on commitment to God, not just each other; (2) they let nothing come between them, not even career or family problems; (3) they drew closer together when their friendship was tested; (4) they remained friends to the end. Jonathan, the prince of Israel, later realized that David, not he, would be the next king (23:17). But that did not weaken his love for David. Jonathan would much rather lose the throne of Israel than lose his closest friend" (NIV, 468).

Ruth and Naomi: But Ruth said, 'Do not urge me to leave you or turn back from following you; for where you go, I will go, and where you lodge, I will lodge. Your people shall be my people, and your God, my God.' (Ruth 1:16, [NASB])

Jesus, Peter, James and John: Six days later, Jesus took with Him Peter, James, and John, and brought them up on a high mountain by themselves. And He was transfigured before them. (Mark 9:2, [NASB])

And He allowed no one to accompany Him, except Peter and James and John the brother of James. (Mark 5:37, [NASB])

As He was sitting on the Mount of Olives opposite the temple, Peter and James and John and Andrew were questioning Him privately. (Mark 13:3, [NASB])

And He took with Him Peter and James and John, and began to be very distressed and troubled. (Mark 14:33, [NASB])

Use the following chart to list the attributes found in each relationship that demonstrates the positive qualities of friendship.

List the attributes and qualities in the friendship in the 3 different groups of friends.	*How might these attributes and qualities translate to 21st century friendships?*
David and Jonathan – 1 Samuel 18-20; 2 Samuel 1	
Ruth and Naomi – The book of Ruth	

Jesus, Peter, James and John – See the various passages listed above.	

THINKING POINT: *There have been times when I have brought up the issue of loneliness in the ministry. Several people have responded at different times that God/Jesus Christ can fill that void. Write your reaction to that statement in the following space.*

_____

_____

_____

_____

_____

_____

_____

_____

_____

_____

Daily Journal: Write about your journey of finding a friend who patterns the attributes and qualities of our Biblical examples.

SUNDAY	
MONDAY	
TUESDAY	

WEDNESDAY	
THURSDAY	
FRIDAY	
SATURDAY	

"Mentoring Younger Women"

Chapter Eleven

Using

Psalm 71:17-18 and Titus 2:3-5

Chapter Eleven

Mentoring Younger Women

According to Wikipedia, the word *mentor* means "a wise and trusted counselor or teacher". I think it's the word "wise" that brings on a feeling of inadequacy when we discuss the subject of mentoring. We all have an inner picture that forms in our mind when we read the definition. Visions of Solomon, and the sisters, Mary and Martha, come to the surface. Few of us would be willing to admit that we fit into the same category with the King of Israel, and the close friends of the Master.

I often wonder where I would be in my journey as a Christian woman had there not been mentors in my life along the way. There are a few that I would like to mention in this chapter as a means of reassuring you that you, too, can be a mentor to young women around you. First, and foremost in my life, my mother was a beacon of light that shone brightly amid many stormy nights. I'm sure she never really comprehended the impact her faith had on my path to belief, and acceptance of Jesus Christ as my personal Savior. It was not so much what she said to me about what she believed, but it was watching her live her faith every day. Her actions in little everyday activities were like megaphones preaching the word. It was how she treated the second graders she taught for thirty-four years. Each one received respect and individual treatment – she loved those children dearly, and they knew it! My mother worked tirelessly to create a wonderful home for my sister and me. She was a single mom, after my dad left, when I was thirteen. Even then, it was my mother's faith that got us through those amazingly scary times. Each night I was a witness to her prayers at the side of her bed. My mother would be on her knees for forty-five minutes to an hour. I knew that she was praying for me, and for my sister. She was a living example of how a human being could rely on the Heavenly Father in all situations.

Along the journey to where I am today there have been numerous women who helped me become the person I am, and will be. In college, it was Dr. Jean Nye, the wife of the pastor of the McComb Presbyterian Church. During our ten years in New Cumberland, PA, I was blessed with several different mentors: Mrs. Sarah Weigle, a member of the church; Mrs. Arlene Boldosser, the wife of our Conference Superintendent; and finally, Mrs. Ethel Lewis, the wife of Dr. Joe Lewis, who was pastor of the Lancaster Church of God at that time.

I'm sure that if each of these women had the opportunity to add comments in this chapter, the first thing they would say is that they didn't realize that they had been a mentor to me. And they would be absolutely correct – they were just living their life as God had led them, and I was watching from the sidelines. How did they treat people? What was their response to difficulties? Were they relying on God, or man for wisdom, and answers to life's questions? Did they remember to pray for things that I mentioned to them? Was I important? As I watched these women in my life, without a doubt there are younger women watching you who need an example of Godly living. It's not so much what you say, as what you do.

Biblical Instruction on Mentoring

In the Army world the women have an organization called Protestant Women of the Chapel – PWOC. It is very similar to our Church of God Women's Ministry, CGWM. One of the offices to be filled within the PWOC is the role of the *Titus 2 Woman*. This is a very prestigious, and honored position. Typically, the office is filled by a seasoned Army wife, who displays the characteristics of the guidelines mentioned in the book of Titus, Chapter 2. Paul wrote a letter to Titus, whom he called "my true child in a common faith" (NASB, 1548). This letter from Paul was written to clarify his instructions for the church in Crete. We can glean from this chapter how we are to conduct ourselves so that we will reflect behavior that aligns itself with Christ.

Older women likewise are to be reverent in their behavior, not malicious gossips nor enslaved to much wine, teaching what is good, *so that they may encourage the young women* [emphasis mine] to love their husbands, to love their children, to be sensible, pure, workers at home, kind, being subject to their own husbands, so that the word of God will not be dishonored (Titus 2:3-5, NASB).

Scripture shows us that the main way we are an encouragement to younger women is through our actions in our daily life. We don't have to meet with them, or have a class to instruct them in the proper way to become a Christian woman. Mark Twain is responsible for the saying, "Actions speak louder than words", but that is only half of his quote. The whole quote reads, "Actions speak louder than words, but not nearly as often." He was a wise man – too many times we talk, and talk, and talk, but our actions do not align with our words. Be an example for those around you – first, to your family, and then to the rest of the world.

Now that I am in my sixties (ouch!) there are two verses in the Psalms that have become extremely important to me. Verses 17 and 18 in Chapter 71 read: "O God, you have taught me from my youth, and I still declare Your wondrous deeds. And even when I am *old and gray,* O God do not forsake me, until *I declare Your strength to this generation, Your power to all who are to come"* (NASB, 754

[emphasis mine]). And, there is a section of Colossians that is now

my "Life Verse". I am on a mission to educate our younger genera-

tion about where to find truth that is the real Truth! Colossians 2:8

says, "See to it that no one takes you captive through philosophy and

empty deception, according to the tradition of men, according to the

elementary principles of the world, rather than according to Christ"

(NASB, 1527). It's one of those verses that all of a sudden jumps out

at you, and it makes you wonder when they added it. It surely wasn't

there the last time you read Colossians, chapter 2!

Mentors of Women in the Bible

Mary Visits Elizabeth

Now at this time Mary arose and went in a hurry to the
hill country, to a city of Judah, and entered the house of
Zacharias and greeted Elizabeth. When Elizabeth heard
Mary's greeting, the baby leaped in her womb; and Elizabeth
was filled with the Holy Spirit. And she cried out with a loud
voice and said, "Blessed are you among women, and blessed
is the fruit of your womb! "And how has it happened to me,

that the mother of my Lord would come to me? "For behold, when the sound of your greeting reached my ears, the baby leaped in my womb for joy. "And blessed is she who believed that there would be a fulfillment of what had been spoken to her by the Lord" (NASB, 1322-1323).

Thinking Point: *What do you notice in these verses that show you that Elizabeth was a mentor to Mary?*

Signposts of Mentoring between Elizabeth and Mary

Naomi's Appeal to Her Daughters-in-law

Then Naomi said to her two daughters-in-law, "Go back! Each of you should go back to your mother's home. May the LORD be as kind to you as you were to me and to our loved ones who have died. May the LORD repay each of you so that you may find security in a home with a husband." When she kissed them goodbye, they began to cry loudly. They said to her, "We are going back with you to your people." But Naomi said, "Go back, my daughters. Why should you go with me? Do I have any more sons in my womb who could be your husbands? Go back, my daughters. Go, because I am too old to get married again. If I said that I still have hope.... And if I had a husband tonight.... And even if I gave birth to sons, would you wait until they grew up and stay single just for them? No, my daughters. My bitterness is much worse than yours because the LORD has sent me so much trouble." They began to cry loudly again. Then Orpah kissed her mother-in-law goodbye, but Ruth held on to her tightly. Naomi said, "Look, your sister-in-law has gone back to her people and to her gods. Go back with your sister-in-law." But Ruth answered, "Don't force me to leave you. Don't make me turn back from following you. Wherever you go, I will go, and wherever you stay, I will stay. Your people will be my people, and your God will be my God. Wherever you die, I will die, and I will be buried there with you. May the LORD strike me down if anything but death separates you and me!" When Naomi saw that Ruth was determined to go with her, she ended the conversation." (Ruth 1:8-18, God's Word Bible).

Ruth and Naomi Talk About Boaz

So Ruth gathered grain in the field until evening. Then she separated the grain from its husks. She had about half a bushel of barley. She picked it up and went into the town, and her mother-in-law saw what she had gathered. Ruth also took out what she had left over from lunch and gave it to Naomi. Her mother-in-law asked her, "Where did you gather grain today? Just where did you work? May the man who paid attention to you be blessed." So Ruth told her mother-in-law about the person with whom she worked. She said, "The man I worked with today is named Boaz." Naomi said to her daughter-in-law, "May the LORD bless him. The LORD hasn't stopped being kind to people—living or dead." Then Naomi told her, "That man is a relative of ours. He is a close relative, one of those responsible for taking care of us." Ruth, who was from Moab, told her, "He also said to me, 'Stay with my younger workers until they have finished the harvest.'" Naomi told her daughter-in-law Ruth, "It's a good idea, my daughter, that you go out to the fields with his young women. If you go to someone else's field, you may be molested." So Ruth stayed with the young women who were working for Boaz. She gathered grain until both the barley harvest and the wheat harvest ended. And she continued to live with her mother-in-law." (Ruth 2:17-23, God's Word Bible).

Naomi's Plan for Ruth's Marriage

Naomi, Ruth's mother-in-law, said to her, "My daughter, shouldn't I try to look for a home that would be good for you? Isn't Boaz, whose young women you've been working with, our relative? He will be separating the barley from its husks on the threshing floor tonight. Freshen up, put on some perfume, dress up, and go down to the threshing floor. Don't let him know that you're there until he's finished eating and drinking. When he lies down, notice the place where he is lying. Then uncover his feet, and lie down there. He will make it clear what you must do." Ruth answered her, "I will do whatever you say." (Ruth 3:1-5, God's Word Bible).

THINKING POINT: *What do you notice in these verses that show you that Naomi was a mentor to Ruth?*

Signposts of Mentoring between Naomi and Ruth

THINKING POINT: *We each have people in our lives that have touched us and made us better or worse. Those who make us better are called mentors. Write about one person in your life that has helped you become the person you are today. Really think about what it was that this person possessed that influenced you to be better.*

_____

_____

_____

_____

_____

_____

_____

_____

_____

Write a prayer asking God to help you be more aware of your opportunities to be a mentor to someone – to influence them not only to be better, but to grow in their walk with Christ. Thank Him for being with you on this journey. And, then trust that He will do what His has promised.

_____

_____

_____

_____

_____

_____

_____

_____

_____

Daily Journal: Choose someone that you would like to mentor, and write each day about something you could do that would influence her for the better.

MONDAY

TUESDAY

WEDNESDAY

THURSDAY

FRIDAY

SATURDAY

SUNDAY

"Mum's the Word"

Chapter Twelve

Using

**Ps 119:37; Pr 4:25; Matt 6:22; Luke 12:2-3;
and various verses from Proverbs and
2 Corinthians12:20**

Chapter Twelve

Mum's the Word

As a child, one of my favorite things to do at my grandmother's farm was to look at her corner cabinet "collectibles". She had several items that I played with regularly: a tiny china tea service, a cast iron stove with all of the implements; a set of black and white dog magnets, and a bronze trio of monkeys – see no evil, hear no evil, and speak no evil. I thought those monkeys were really funny, and I was always getting my sister and cousins to line up in front of our parents and grandparents as those monkeys. I realize now what a statement that bronze paperweight was making – actually, it had a very scripturally based message! In this chapter, which covers the issue of confidentiality, we will take a look at each one of those monkeys individually. When we discuss the subject of confidentiality, often we just focus on the importance of watching our mouths, and not sharing what we have heard. But, it's much more than that.

There is a children's song that reminds us of those three monkeys. It has several verses:

"Oh, be careful little eyes what you see. Oh, be careful little eyes what you see. For the Father up above is looking down with love, so be careful little eyes what you see.

Oh, be careful little ears what you hear. Oh, be careful little ears what you hear. For the Father up above is looking down with love, so be careful little ears what you hear.

Oh, be careful little mouth what you say. Oh, be careful little mouth what you say. For the Father up above is looking down with love, so be careful little mouth what you say."

Isn't it amazing how children's songs can carry really deep scriptural messages? Christians should start the day singing this song as a reminder of how to conduct themselves throughout the day.

We'll start by looking at the "see no evil" monkey, and the verse that talks about being careful what we see. Our eyes are an amazing part of the body. When I think about how the eye functions, it makes my brain hurt! How does it bring all of the colors, or what allows the eye to show movement? It is an incredible creation of God. The eye sees everything – unfortunately, all of those things are not good.

There are times that our eyes cannot avoid seeing things that are outside of the wishes of our Father. Unfortunately, there are instances where we choose to use our eyes in a way that dishonors God. One of the problems surrounding confidentiality deals with being too interested in seeing what is going on around us. Most of what occurs is none of our business. The word for this problem is "curiosity." The terms "nosey body", and "snoop" have been used to label people with this malady. The television show "Bewitched" had the perfect example of this type of person. The neighbor, Gladys, was always looking out of her window to discover the secrets of the Stevens household. Her eyes were not being used the way God intended them to be used. We should learn to respect each person's right to confidentiality, and keep our eyes where they belong.

What does Scripture say about...?

The Eye

Matthew 6:22-23

The eye is the lamp of the body. If your eyes are good, your whole body will be full of light. But if your eyes are bad, your whole body will be full of darkness. If then the light within you is darkness, how great is that darkness (NIV, 1569).

One interpretation of the scripture from Matthew's gospel has to do with the perfect working of the eye. If you have a good eye, then you will be able to see light, and all of those things around you. But, if your eye is not functioning properly, then you will live in a dark world, not being able to see light and objects. I believe Matthew had another meaning imbedded in those two verses. *Read them over again, and write about what he might also have been saying to those who heard, or read his words.*

> *What else might Matthew have been trying to say in Chapter 6,*
>
> *verses 22 and 23?*

<u>Psalm 119:37</u>

Turn my eyes away from worthless things; preserve my life according to your word (NIV, 927).

The writer of Psalm 119, verse 37, was pleading with God to assist him in achieving something that was not possible in his own power. It is easy to hear the need of the writer to remove the desire to continue looking on things that were not according to God's word.

What we must realize is that allowing God to have control over the various parts of our body is the only way we can resist the temptation to use them for our own gain. For some people it is a daily struggle to avoid "intrusively looking" into others lives.

What do you think God might be saying to you through verse 37?

Proverbs 4:25

Let your eyes look straight ahead, fix your gaze directly before you (NIV, 965).

When I read this verse I thought about horses, and how there are certain times that the horse will wear "blinders". The purpose of this apparatus is to keep the horse focused on what is directly in front of him, and not be distracted by what might be going on around him. Another illustration that seems appropriate is the gymnast on a balance beam. The only way for the gymnast to stay perfectly balanced is to stay focused on a specific object directly in front of him or her. If the focus moves away from the object, balance is lost, and disaster can happen. There are so many possible distractions that can take our sight away from what is good and true. Those negative possibilities cause us to lose our focus, and fall away from God's intended purpose for us.

When we intentionally encourage our eyes to see into the private lives of others, what can be some of the results of that choice?

The Ear *Luke 12: 2-3*

There is nothing concealed that will not be disclosed, or hidden that will not be made known. What you have said in the dark will be heard in the daylight, and what you have whispered in the ear in the inner rooms will be proclaimed from the roof (NIV, 1693).

A game that was a lot of fun to play during indoor recess was "Gossip". I'm sure that you've all played it before. The person in charge makes up a sentence, and whispers it very quietly into the ear of the first person. Then each person whispers what has been heard into the next person's ear. When the message has made its way to the end of the line, the last person repeats what the he believes was the original sentence. Most often the last person's sentence bears no resemblance to the original message. It was always so much fun to finally get to listen to what the last person heard. And it was always best when the final message was really messed up.

As much fun as that game of "Gossip" is, in reality, messages that are passed from one person to another invariably become distorted along the way. This can be devastating when the story deals with someone's life. Even when you are just relaying information, you can innocently convey bad information. One very poignant illustration happened to me while we were living in New Cumberland, PA. I was having major surgery that involved removing tissue, and replacing that tissue with implants. I had a severe case of fibrocystic disease, and the surgeons felt it was best to proceed with the operation. This was major surgery, and I was in the hospital for almost a week. Naturally, word spread that I was in the Harrisburg Hospital, and had many visitors. I gave those friends who came to visit permission to share my need for "recovery prayers".

Six months after the surgery, I saw an acquaintance in downtown New Cumberland. She informed me that the story was being passed that I had breast cancer, and was dying. My immediate response was to laugh! But, as I thought about this more, I realized there had to be many people out there thinking I was dying, and I had no way to tell them differently. I still don't know how my surgery to remove tissue ballooned into people being told that I had terminal cancer.

I am positive that however that story got started, it was done very innocently, and for my best interest. This is just one case of how careful we must be about sharing information. It's also important to understand that what you HEAR may not necessarily be truth! Unless the information comes from the original source, it is a must to check out the message before passing it on.

Frequently, I get emails stating that someone is going to *do something*, and I must forward this message to everyone I know! I have learned to use *snopes.com* before forwarding any email of that nature. We are so easily led to believe what we hear before checking for ourselves what the truth might be. Each of us must guard against taking as truth everything we hear. A good rule of thumb: **Always check with the original source before passing along a story. Remember: there is a fine line between sharing a concern, and gossip. This goes for the speaker, and the listener.**

Write about a time in your life that you have been caught up in a situation like the one above. Did you hear something, and share it without checking its validity, or have things been said about you that were not true?

verse 3: "What you have said in the dark will be heard in the daylight, and what you have whispered in the ear in the inner rooms will be proclaimed from the roofs."

The Mouth (Gossip) – After reading each selection from the book of Proverbs, write a paraphrase (putting it into your own words) showing what the writer was trying to explain to you.

Proverbs 11:13

A gossip betrays a confidence, but a trustworthy man keeps a secret (NIV, 976).

Proverbs 16:28

A perverse man stirs up dissension, and a gossip separates close friends (NIV, 985).

Proverbs 18:8

The words of a gossip are like choice morsels; they go down to a man's inmost parts (NIV, 987).

Proverbs 20:19

A gossip betrays a confidence; so avoid a man who talks too much (NIV, 991).

Proverbs 26:20

Without wood a fire goes out; without gossip a quarrel dies down (NIV, 1003).

Proverbs 26:22

The words of a gossip are like choice morsels; they go down to a man's inmost parts (NIV, 1003).

Paul had great concern about the Church in Corinth. The society of this city was greatly diverse, which created special circumstances and temptations for the new fellowship of believers there. There were many different "truths" being tossed around which caused dissention, gossip, and disunity. The verse from 2 Corinthians that you will read demonstrates Paul's immediate concern that the believers avoid specific pitfalls that cause division among the church. He targeted the following behaviors as inhibitors of unity: "quarreling, jealousy, outbursts of anger, factions, slander, *gossip* [emphasis mine], arrogance, and disorder" (NIV, 1899). Read the following verses and then reflect on your experience with the people of God (your Church). Have these behaviors been a part of creating disunity within the believers?

2 Corinthians 12:20

For I am afraid that when I come I may not find you as I want you to be, and you may not find me as you want me to be. I fear that there may be quarreling, jealousy, outbursts of anger, factions, slander, gossip, arrogance and disorder (NIV, 1899).

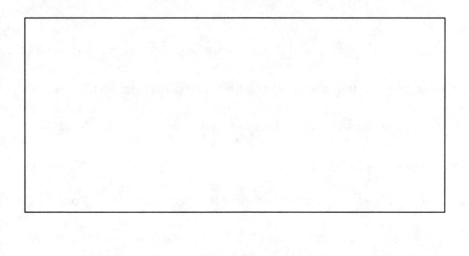

As the wife of a Pastor you will be told many things that fall into the category of "confidences". Some may come from your husband, but most will be told to you by members of the congregation. You will **_see_**, and **_hear_** many things as you continue to serve God in His various callings. What you do with those things will be very important to the success of your ministry with your husband. One of the greatest gifts that you can give to your husband is your ability to be trustworthy with what you know. I learned to act very surprised when asked if I knew about some bit of news concerning a member of the congregation.

There will be those times when you may have to be very blunt with some people. Maya Angelou, an African American poet and writer, once spoke about dealing with negative people, and people who loved to talk about others. She shared that she finally decided she had to be very straightforward with those people. When they would begin to try to bring her into their participation in negativity and gossip, she would very clearly tell them that she did not want to continue in that conversation. That's the only way some folks get the message.

Daily Journal – *Each day write a prayer for someone you know that has a problem with the lack of confidentiality – it might even be you! Eliminate the names to protect the innocent!*

Monday
Tuesday

Wednesday

Thursday

Friday

Saturday

Sunday

"Dealing with Tragedy in the Church"

Chapter Thirteen

Using

1 Corinthians 10:13; Ecclesiastes 3:1-8;
Job 2:11,13; Luke 18:18-29; Numbers 13;
Ruth; Genesis 27:1-10

Chapter Thirteen

Dealing With Tragedy in the Church

"**N**o temptation has overtaken you but such as is common to man; and God is faithful, who will not allow you to be tempted beyond what you are able, but with the temptation will provide the way of escape also, so that you will be able to endure it" (1 Cor. 10:13, [NASB]). How often have you heard someone paraphrase the preceding verse: "God will not give me more than I can bear", or glibly say, "God said that He would never give me more than I could handle. I wish He didn't have such a high opinion of me"? We have certainly taken liberties in interpreting 1 Corinthians 10:13. Paul was writing about the temptations that surround us every day, but we have used this verse many times to include burdens that come our way.

While you and your husband minister to God's people there will be a myriad of emotions that you must encounter. Joel and I learned very early in his pastoral calling that tragedy can cause great anguish. He was serving a small Methodist Church in Rudolph, Ohio. Joel was in his first year at Winebrenner Theological Seminary in Findlay, Ohio, and I was a senior at Findlay College. He received a call from a member of our church that a two and a half year old child from our congregation had been struck by a car, and was in the emergency room in Bowling Green. By the time we arrived in the Emergency Room, the little girl had already been moved to a hospital in Toledo. Soon after Joel and I made the trip to Toledo, the family was told that Shelley had died. How do you help at this time? What do you say to a grandfather who witnessed the accident, and couldn't prevent it? How do you comfort a father who was drunk the night before, totaled his car, and walked away uninjured? What words could we share as the family looked to the two of us for answers, and there were no answers? The only comfort we found to give was to hold their hands, put our arms around them, and be silent. We sent wordless prayers to the Father in Heaven who understood the pain.

Throughout our forty years of ministry we have witnessed members of our flock experience unimaginable grief: pregnancies that ended in miscarriage, or as a stillborn infant; a terminal diagnosis; ruptured marriages; the end of lives well-spent; a life that ends far too soon; a job lost; and the list could go on forever. As caregivers, these tragic circumstances begin to weigh on your heart and soul. There can be an emptiness that takes root, and there is nothing left to give to those who turn to you seeking comfort and answers.

Ecclesiastes 3:1-8 has been quoted so often in times such as those mentioned above. Popular music even used the theme from these verses. In 1959, Pete Seeger wrote a song, "Turn, Turn, Turn", that was completely from Ecclesiastes 3:1-8, except for the last six words. It was released in 1962, on the album "The Bitter and The Sweet", by Columbia Records. It is not hard to understand why

Seeger would put together a song using these "lyrics" at this partic-

ular time. The world was experiencing an amazing amount of grief

during uncertain days. The eight verses from chapter 3, bring com-

fort during years of pain and uncertainty.

A Time for Everything

There is a time for everything, and a season for every activity
under heaven:
a time to be born and a time to die, a time to plant and a time
to uproot,
a time to kill and a time to heal, a time to tear down and a
time to build,
a time to weep and a time to laugh, a time to mourn and a
time to dance,
a time to scatter stones and a time to gather them, a time to
embrace and a time to refrain,
a time to search and a time to give up, a time to keep and a
time to throw away,
a time to tear and a time to mend, a time to be silent and a
time to speak,
a time to love and a time to hate, a time for war and a time
for peace(NASB, 864).

Each one of the verses from Ecclesiastes 3:1-8, speaks to those

who must deal with tragedy. These words should be required study for every person that seeks to minister to God's people. There is a "time" for each feeling, response, and reaction – God's time, not our time.

Pitfalls to Avoid

1.) *Acknowledge that you don't possess all of the answers/ explanations*.

When confronted with someone's grief, the majority of people feel a compelling need to restore a sense of well-being to those who are affected by the event. This is a God-given, and a God-created reaction. The desire is to "make things better", but, unfortunately, in our attempts to help, we often stumble, and fall flat on our faces. I cannot count the number of times I have overheard some "kind soul" trying to bring words of comfort to grief stricken people, only to have to mop up the mess afterwards. Comments such as: "Well, God needed another angel for His choir"; "You can always have another child"; "It's for the best – he/she was really suffering"; "At least he/she lived a full life". The old saying, "If you can't say something nice, don't say anything at all", holds true in this case, also. The best response during times of grief is no response. Listening to the person's grief with a closed mouth is usually the best medicine.

Scriptural Example: Job 2:11 – "When Job's three friends, Eliphaz the Temanite, Bildad the Shuhite and Zophar the Naamathite, heard about all the troubles that had come upon him, they set out from their homes and met together by agreement to go and sympathize with him and comfort him" (NIV, 739). The following verses add that these three friends stayed with Job for seven days and nights. But the most important information is found in verse 13: "***No one said a word to him, because they saw how great his suffering was*** [emphasis mine]." If we read no further, then we would be very impressed with Job's friends. They expressed great caring and empathy for all of Job's trials. However, as we read through the next chapters concerning the plight of Job, his friends did not remain silent. Each man told Job why he was experiencing this tribulation. Their opportunity to comfort Job had come to an abrupt end. We must also realize that in an effort to comfort, words can bring more pain.

2.) ***Resist becoming emotionally involved.***

This is one of my most difficult areas to keep from falling into a pit! My tendency is to become so involved in someone else's tragedy that it begins to affect my own life. There are times when I have a hard time separating myself from the emotions generated by the event. Even passing an accident on the highway can create a sense of worry about those involved in the traffic incident. It takes great effort on my part to be able to let go of the feelings of concern that I experience. I have had to work hard at developing a "safe" boundary when it comes to dealing with tragedy.

Scriptural Example: Luke 18:18-29

A certain ruler asked him, "Good teacher, what must I do to inherit eternal life?" "Why do you call me good?" Jesus answered. "No one is good—except God alone. You know the commandments: 'Do not commit adultery, do not murder, do not steal, do not give false testimony, honor your father and mother." "All these I have kept since I was a boy," he said. When Jesus heard this, he said to him, "You still lack one thing. Sell everything you have and give to the poor, and you will have treasure in heaven. Then come, follow me." When he heard this, he became very sad, because he was a man of great wealth. Jesus looked at him and said, "How hard it is for the rich to enter the kingdom of God! Indeed, it is easier for a camel to go through the eye of a needle than for a rich man to enter the kingdom of God." Those who heard this asked, "Who then can be saved?" Jesus replied, "What is impossible with men is possible with God." Peter said to him, "We have left all we had to follow you!" "I tell you the truth," Jesus said to them, "no one who has left home or wife or brothers or parents or children for the sake of the kingdom of God will fail to receive many times as much in this age and, in the age to come, eternal life" (NIV, 1703).

Jesus was always able to cut to the heart of every question that was asked of Him. The rich young man, mentioned in the Gospel of Luke, desired to know how he could inherit eternal life. This is the ultimate question each person must ask. We have Jesus' response in verse 20 and 22, and we also have the reaction of the young ruler in verse 23. Sadness overcame the young man because he realized the cost was more than he was willing to pay. We have no record of any attempt by Jesus to convince the man to follow through with an act of relinquishing all of his goods to the poor. Jesus was able to walk away from the anguish. Don't misunderstand me! We are to do our utmost to help those experiencing pain and suffering, and to sympathize with them! BUT – we must avoid taking on the responsibility of solving the issues for each situation. For our own emotional stability as a ministry team, we must keep a healthy separation between the tragedy of members of our flock, and our own personal lives.

3.) *Keep a balance between minimizing and catastrophising the event.*

It would be good to visualize a scale, or a see-saw. When viewing an event, there must be a balanced reaction by those who minister to the people experiencing a tragedy. There are three possible ways to react to a given situation:

    a.) Minimize the event: A percentage of people will always respond to tragic events by down-playing what has occurred. This type of person usually relays a personal story that is much worse than the present situation. And a typical message of comfort would be, "Just be glad it wasn't worse!" This is never a time to relay stories of "similar or worse experiences". I can easily picture Jonah in this category! He would whine about being tossed overboard, share graphic details about the insides of the belly of a whale, and complain that God caused the vine to die that had provided him shade. I'm convinced that according to Jonah no one could have had it worse!

b.) ***Make the event a catastrophe***: You've seen these people in action! There is the presence of frenzied activity, and an air of hysteria. This generates a large amount of stress, and expends an unnecessary amount of energy. The caregiver in this scenario becomes the center of attention. The message of comfort sounds like the following: "I can't help you deal with this right now – it's just too much to bear!" The care-givers must realize that they are outside of the event, and their function is to bring a sense of calm with them. The biblical characters that I picture in this category are the twelve spies of Moses from Numbers 13. The picture they shared of the Promised Land was out of focus and much exaggerated. They spoke of giants in the land of great strength, and that the "land devours those living in it" (NIV, 215). The spies compared themselves to grasshoppers in the eyes of the inhabitants of the land of Canaan. It took the calm attitude of Caleb and Joshua to convey the true picture of what existed in the future home of the Israelites. Unfortunately, God withheld the promised territory from the people for another forty years.

c.) *A balanced approach to the event*: These are the people that I want around me when I am experiencing a tragic event in my life. I have had my fair share of types "a" and "b", and I'm sure that I have been guilty of being both of those at times myself! The principle characteristic of the type "c" person is the ability to bring a presence of calmness. This person has a clear picture of, and response to the event. The message of comfort from this person would be like the following: "I am sorry that you must deal with this right now. I will be here if you need me." Ruth exemplifies the spirit of calm in times of tragic events. Her demeanor in each situation with Naomi illustrates the benefit of seeing clearly, and responding appropriately. The dilemma facing Ruth was dire:

a.) Ruth's husband had died.

b.) She decided to leave her homeland, and follow her mother-in-law to a strange country.

c.) Ruth would be considered an enemy in the land of her mother-in-law.

d.) She submitted to Naomi's guidance concerning a man she did not know.

e.) Ruth's future was in the hands of other people.

4.) ***Don't allow yourself to be triangulated among those experiencing the event.***

A triangle is a geometric shape that possesses three sides. It is a wonderful shape, and the triangle was one of my favorite instruments to play in elementary school. Being part of a "triangle of people" can lead to an unfortunate and uncomfortable involvement. Caregivers can find themselves caught between two people, or two sides of a situation. Pastors and wives of pastors should take great care to avoid taking sides during disputes or tragic events. It's best to remain neutral when disagreements occur. It is not uncommon when people are in the midst of emotional upheaval for misunderstandings to happen. In the death of a loved one, even planning for a funeral can bring out the worst in many of us. It is important for those ministering to the family to avoid being drawn into the decision-making moments – invariably someone is not going to be happy!!

Scriptural Example: Genesis 27:1-10

Now it came about, when Isaac was old and his eyes were too dim to see, that he called his older son Esau and said to him, "My son." And he said to him, "Here I am." Isaac said, "Behold now, I am old and I do not know the day of my death. Now then, please take your gear, your quiver, and your bow, and go out to the field and hunt game for me; and prepare a savory dish for me such as I love, and bring it to me that I may eat, so that my soul may bless you before I die." Rebekah was listening while Isaac spoke to his son Esau. So when Esau went to the field to hunt for game to bring home, Rebekah said to her son Jacob, "Behold, I heard your father speak to your brother Esau, saying 'Bring me some game and prepare a savory dish for me, that I may eat, and bless you in the presence of the Lord before my death.' "Now therefore, my son, listen to me as I command you. Go now to the flock and bring me two choice young goats from there, that I may prepare them as a savory dish for your father, such as he loves. Then you shall bring it to your father that he may eat, so that he may bless you before his death (NASB, 34).

As you read the passage, could you see the triangle forming? The family of Isaac is about to experience a very tragic event – the death of the head of the household. The triangle consists of Isaac, Rebekah, and Esau. Because of Rebekah's decision to intervene in the gift of the blessing to Jacob, brother was set against brother, and Jacob was forced to run away to save his life. The moment we allow ourselves to become part of a triangle, we cannot predict what future tragedies may occur. No one can pull you into a triangulated position unless you allow them to do so. Before becoming involved with any tragedy in the church family, ask God to be your Guide and Protection. Ask for His wisdom in dealing with the varied circumstances that will surround your ministry to the family and friends. Then you must listen, and follow His instructions.

5.) *Realize that you can't heal every situation.* Of all of the pitfalls you've read about, this is the easiest one to fall into most often. We have a tremendous need as caregivers to bring every story to a happy ending. In a "Disney" world, that is possible. However, in real life, happy endings require time and hard work. It doesn't take long for those in the ministry to realize that sometimes their best is not enough. It is frustrating to face the reality of "failure". I put the word in quotation marks because that is the perception of the caregiver. We find ourselves wanting to have everything tied up neatly with a bow, bringing closure to the event. Then we can place it on a shelf, and put a checkmark indicating that the "mission" was complete.

Scriptural Example: Matthew 8:28-34

> When He came to the other side into the country of the Gadarenes, two men who were demon-possessed met Him as they were coming out of the tombs. They were so extremely violent that no one could pass by that way. And they cried out, saying, "What business do we have with each other, Son of God? Have you come here to torment us before the time?" Now there was a herd of many swine feeding at a distance from them. The demons began to entreat Him, saying, "If You are going to cast us out, send us into the herd of swine." And He said to them, "Go!" And they came out and went into the swine, and the whole herd rushed down the steep bank into the sea and perished in the waters. The herdsmen ran away, and went to the city and reported everything, including what had happened to the demoniacs. And behold, the whole city came out to meet Jesus; and when they saw Him, they implored Him to leave their region" (NASB, 1253).

There were not many times that Jesus received the reaction He did from these villagers. Fear encompassed the people of the city, and they wanted Him gone immediately. Jesus had just assisted this community with ridding them of a public nuisance – two demon-possessed men who were violent, and were disrupting the everyday activities of the people. Most of us would assume that the reaction of the people would be gratitude. The focal point of this scripture passage is in looking at the response of Jesus to the request for Him to leave their presence. There is no record of Him trying to explain what had happened, or to remove their feeling of fear about what they had heard and seen. In the next verse, Chapter 9:1, Jesus gets into a boat, crosses the water, and went to minister in another city. The wisdom of Jesus teaches us that there are times when you must walk away from events, and allow those involved to figure things out for themselves. And, just like our Master, you must be able to relinquish your desire to heal every problem.

WHAT IS THE ANSWER TO SUSTAINING STRENGTH THROUGHOUT THE LENGTH OF THE MINISTRY?

Isaiah 40:31 clearly defines how to maintain your strength when circumstances drain every ounce of endurance your body possesses: "Yet those who wait for the Lord **will gain** new strength [emphasis mine]; they will mount up with wings like eagles, they will run and not get tired, they will walk and not become weary" (NASB, 932). If we try to do everything in our own ability, then we will run out of the physical resources necessary to complete the mission. 1 Peter 4:11 states: "Whoever speaks, is to do so as one who is speaking the utterances of God; **whoever serves is to do so as one who is serving by the strength which God supplies;** *so that in all things God may be glorified through Jesus Christ* [emphasis mine], to whom belongs the glory and dominion forever and ever" (NASB, 1577). Scripture very clearly teaches us that our strength comes from God, and when faced with ministering to His Church we must depend on Him alone to bring comfort. Our "well" will run dry without His Presence to continually replenish the supply of strength we need.

The Apostle Paul experienced the presence of God's strength throughout his ministry to the new Christians. He knew the importance of depending on the Lord to replenish and restore him so he could continue to bring the Good News, and comfort to the new believers. In Philippians 4:13, Paul shares with all of us what he believes is the central answer to avoiding becoming weary: "I CAN DO ALL THINGS THROUGH HIM WHO STRENGTHENS ME" (NASB, 1525 [emphasis mine]).

If you gain nothing else from this chapter, then it is my prayer that you take with you the central message that God will always be there with you as you minister during tragic events in the life of the church you serve. You can try to do this on your own strength, but eventually the ability to continue will end. The promise of God is to fill you with His power, and strength to face the challenges. "Come to Me, all who are weary and heavy-laden, and I will give you rest" (NASB, 1258).

Daily Journal – *As I look back over the years of ministering to the needs of people, I realize that I didn't always take the time to ask God's presence to help me have the strength to respond to the individual situations. I would find myself drained, and then ask God to restore me. The Pennsylvania Dutch would call that "putting the cart before the horse", and they would be correct! Reflect on your ministry to God's people, and write about how you have "felt and dealt" with those situations.*

Monday
Tuesday
Wednesday

Thursday

Friday

Saturday

Sunday

Acknowledgments

First, and foremost, I thank my Heavenly Father for giving me the inner nudging to write this book, <u>Nobody Told Me</u>. I felt His presence every day as I sat down to write the words that eventually became chapters. God has sustained me throughout my life, in every situation, and in every transition. Without Him, I could have accomplished nothing.

Next, I want to acknowledge Sue Sansom, and thank her for listening to that small, still voice of God as He nudged her, also. Sue emailed me in the fall of 2009, and asked if I had ever considered writing a book for pastors' wives. She had no way of knowing that I had recently begun writing the first chapter of that book! Her email was the confirmation that God was in this book!

I want to thank my family – husband, children, and my sisters-in-law. I have been encouraged by them to put my journey as the wife of a Pastor/Army Chaplain in book form. My husband and children were used as examples of what can go on in the life of the parsonage, and I appreciate their willingness to allow the readers access to their sometimes embarrassing moments. I am proud of my children, and their continuing walk as Christians, as I watch them minister to God's people, also.

Lastly, to my friends who have watched me at my seat on the second floor of Winebrenner Theological Seminary, I want to express my gratitude for supporting my desire to write this book. Not only did you support my desire, but many times helped me think of Scripture passages, and suggested topics I might want to include. Several of you helped to edit the book: Jeannine Grimm; Ruth Whitaker, Kelly Bullington (daughter), and Joel Cocklin (husband).

Bibliography

Hilderbrand, Karen Mitzo and Kim Mitzo Thompson, "Oh Be Careful Little Eyes". 1999. http://www.childbiblesongs.com/song-12-be-careful-little-eyes.shtml [accessed July 9, 2010].

Holy Bible: The archaeological study Bible in the New International Version. 2005. Grand Rapids: Zondervan.

Holy Bible: God's Word. Database, 2008. WORDsearch Corp.

Holy Bible: New American Standard Version. 2002. La Habra, CA: Zondervan.

Hurley, John and Ronnie Wilkins. 1968. *Son of a preacher man.* Performed by Dusty Springfield and others. Atlanta Records.

Lotz, Anne Graham. 2007. Untitled Lecture, Protestant Women of the Chapel, Fort Bragg, NC. October 6.

Nouwen, Henry J.M. 1990. *The road to daybreak: a spiritual journey.* New York: Doubleday Dell Publishing Group, Inc.

Walter Reed Army Institute of Research. 2007. *Helping You and Your Family Transition from Deployments.* Washington, DC: http://www.armyg1.armymil/dcs/docs/Operation%20 Ready%20Post-Deployment%20Battlemind%20 Training%20for%20spouses.pgf [accessed September 14, 2010].

Winfrey, Oprah. "Oprah Talks to Maya Angelou". *The Oprah Magazine* [December 2000], http://www.oprah.com/omagazine/Oprah-interviews-Maya-Angelou [accessed July 20, 2010.

Seeger, Pete. 1962. *Turn, turn, turn*. Performed by Pete Seeger and others. Columbia Records.